QUARTERBACKING

Happy Birthday Marc

Joe Theismann

1 Oct 1983

Joe Theismann

QUARTERBACKING

ST. MARTIN'S PRESS, NEW YORK

QUARTERBACKING. Revised Second Edition. Copyright © 1975, 1983 by Joe
Theismann. All rights reserved. Printed in the United States of America. No part
of this book may be used or reproduced in any manner whatsoever without
written permission except in the case of brief quotations embodied in critical
articles or reviews. For information, address St. Martin's Press, 175 Fifth Avenue,
New York, N.Y. 10010.

Library of Congress Cataloging in Publication Data

Theismann, Joe.
  Quarterbacking.

  1. Quarterback (Football) 2. Football. I. Title.
GV951.3.T47   1983   796.332′25   83-9669
ISBN 0-312-65871-0 (pbk.)

10 9 8 7 6 5 4 3 2

CONTENTS

ACKNOWLEDGMENTS

The author is indebted to his parents—for providing him with the opportunity to play ball; to his coaches—for their time, their talent, their trust; to his wife, Cheryl, for being wonderful and understanding.

INTRODUCTION

If you asked football coaches to enumerate the physical qualities of the ideal quarterback, they could spew out dimensions and sizes that boggle the mind.

Joe Theismann, Notre Dame's premier quarterback in the late 60s and early 70s, defied all of the computerized physical stature requisites.

Far from brawny, Joe possessed an innate quickness coupled with tremendous dexterity of foot, hand, and mind. He was the true matador. Knowing full well that a little man must prove that he can play, Joe became a great student of the game. His knowledge on the field as a player was more that of a player-coach. For him, practices were pressured moments to refine techniques, polish skills, understand the opponents, and devise his game plan for the attack. With an affinity for work, knowledge of what to perfect, and perhaps most of all, belief in himself as his greatest talent, he was, is, and will always be, a winner!

Joe Theismann's ability to learn from his teachers, particularly his backfield coach, Tom Pagna, his analytical ability to glean the best of other players, his adept creativity in fitting the best to his own style, all contribute to this comprehensive insight into quarterbacking.

Indeed, a whole picture of understanding comes through clearly as one reads the whys and hows of this book. Pictures, explanations, personal insights, and years of experience are packed into loaded sentences to produce a superb book of instruction.

My staff and I were proud of Joe's gridiron accomplishments. I dare say these have yet to reach a peak. Now he makes me proud again with his in-depth critique of "quarterbacking." This further demonstration of excellence comes as no surprise.

It looks to me as if Joe Theismann is in the act of completing yet another long pass.

Sincerely,

ARA PARSEGHIAN

QUARTERBACKING

Photo by Dick Darcey, *Washington Post*

1 Do You Want To Be a Quarterback?

The quarterback spot is the key position in an offensive attack. In today's game the quarterback must be first, last, and always an athlete. Your leadership ability, poise, and confidence must be above average; you must have a competitive spirit, loyalty, and dedication to the understanding and study of the game. You have to possess the gifts of an athlete in your dexterity of foot and hand, general quickness, and coordination.

Since today's game of football is almost balanced equally between the run and the pass, possessing these assets will make you a more complete quarterback. The better the original athletic gifts, the better a team leader you will be.

Photo by Nate Fine

Getting instructions from Coach Gibbs.

A dedicated quarterback prides himself not only on the number of touchdown passes he throws, but also on the type of game he has called. Sure, he might have thrown an interception or two, but a great quarterback can overcome setbacks and lead his team to victory.

To play well, you must have dedication and talent, for success depends on the degree of talent and time you are willing to spend on the game. Size isn't the all-important factor. You don't have to be 6′5″ or 210 pounds to be a great quarterback. Being tall may enable you to see over the on-rushing linesmen, but it is the job of your offensive line to create passing lanes for you to throw through. (By "passing lanes" I mean a clear line of vision between you and your receivers.) Never use your size as an excuse.

Believing in yourself is a very important part of playing quarterback—you must feel that you are the best at your position. If you don't believe in yourself, you shouldn't expect your teammates to believe in you. I'm considered small for professional football, but I feel I can play with the best of them.

It is one thing to feel you are the best. The next step is to go out and prove it! This is where communication plays a big part in the molding of a quarterback. You must be able to communicate not only with the coach, but with your teammates. You must be respected by the men you play football for and with. Always give your best and you will gain that respect.

Communication between you and your coach is of the utmost importance for a team to function properly. This relationship must be developed on the practice field in order to carry over into the game. A lot of things happen fast in a game, and you and the coach must be able to relate to each other quickly and easily. You will meet two kinds of coaches during your career. One type will criticize you and be very tough with you in front of your teammates. He is doing this in order to rally the team behind you against the "ogre." The other coach is a man who will very seldom criticize you in front of others. He'll take you aside, explain to you what you are doing wrong, and then send you back to do your job properly. You may prefer one type of coach over the other, but throughout your career you *will* meet both.

As a quarterback, you are constantly under pressure, and it comes from all sides—your coach, your teammates, your fans, and even yourself. You have to learn to

The joy of victory: presenting Coach Gibbs a game ball after a win over the Eagles.

Photo by Nate Fine

cope with it. Everyone is scared or nervous before a game—it's evidence of the pressure you put on yourself.

Under all this pressure people will make mistakes. If a lineman misses a block or a receiver runs a wrong pattern, very few people will know. If you make a move in the wrong direction, the world will know. It's part of being a quarterback. But you also get most of the congratulations if your team does well. Telling the world whether you were a champ or a chump is the job of the media—radio, press, and TV. If you don't play well, you can't expect these men to cover up for you. They are doing their job just as you are doing yours. So just because you don't agree with a statement on TV or in the newspapers, don't criticize the media. Accept the comments with good grace. You may be able to learn from them.

Anyone with talent who is willing to work can become a professional quarterback. When you become a professional, all of your hard work will have paid off. Imagine playing with and against some of those players whose pictures are on posters in your bedroom! This is just a part of the thrill of playing professional football.

While you are working toward becoming a professional, set goals for yourself, not just in football, but in the rest of your life as well. If you make them as difficult as possible, you'll always be trying your best. Even if you fall a little short on some of them, the time and effort put into reaching these goals will have made you a better person and quarterback.

When I entered the University of Notre Dame my goal was to be the best quarterback ever to play there. I could have settled for just making the team, but I wanted to be the best. At the time I set this goal, I was 5'10" tall and weighed 148 pounds, and my goal seemed almost impossible. I went ahead anyway, and worked harder and harder. There were times when I wanted to quit, as in my freshman year when I walked onto the field my first day of practice and there were eight other quarterbacks. It would have been easier to take a back seat and just be second string, but I didn't want that. I wanted to be Number One. I may *not* have been the best quarterback Notre Dame ever had, but I believe that working toward a difficult goal made me a better quarterback and a better human being.

So when you set your goals, be prepared to work as hard as you can to achieve them. It will all be worth it in the end. Developing a love for the game will make all the hard work seem more like fun.

2 Flexibility Exercises

The following stretching movements should be done slowly. Bouncing and jerking motions cause a reflex action in muscles that make them tighten and resist stretching. This type of stretching is self-defeating and can even cause injury.

Hold your body in the position of maximum stretch for five to eight seconds, and then relax and repeat. You should feel a tightness in the area that you are stretching, but never force a muscle to stretch to the point where it is painful. Instead, concentrate on relaxing the muscle and stretch it carefully.

Use the following list of stretching exercises to select six to eight movements to be done every time you work out. You can switch these occasionally for variety and use any that you may already know as well. A ten-minute stretching period should be included before any weightlifting or running workout.

Hamstring / Groin / Hip

Lift leg straight up and lower to opposite hand . . . Pause and return . . . Keep other leg stationary. . . . Repeat to other side.

Hamstring / Abdomen / Hip

Raise legs upward and lower to one side . . . Pause and
return . . . Repeat to other side. . . . Legs must be straight
throughout.

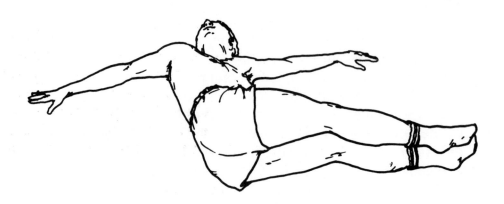

Hip / Abdomen / Shoulders

Slowly lift straight legs over to the ground . . . Pause and
return. . . . Keep legs together.

Hip / Abdomen / Shoulders / Groin

Slowly lift straight legs over to the ground . . . Pause and return. . . . Keep legs straddled.

Hamstring / Groin / Shoulders

Lower head to knee . . . Pause and return . . . Repeat to other side. . . . Keep both legs straight.

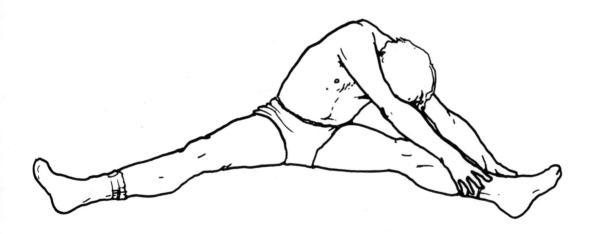

Groin/Lower Back/Hamstring

Wide straddle . . . Lower chest to ground . . . Keep legs straight . . . Pause and return.

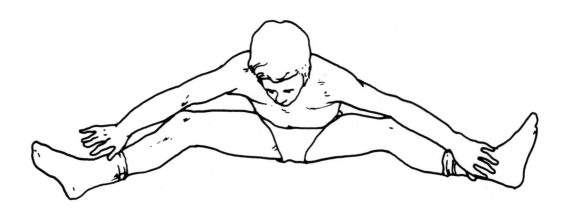

Hamstring / Lower Back / Shoulders / Abdomen

Slowly lower head to knees . . . Keep legs straight . . . Arms and shoulders stretched . . . Pause and return.

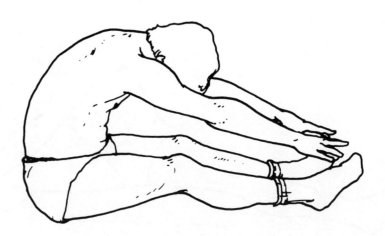

Hamstring

Raise straight leg to vertical . . . Pause and return . . .
Repeat to other side. . . . Keep other leg straight.

Quads / Back

Kneel . . . Roll back to the ground . . . Pause and return. . . . Use hands to side for assistance.

Hamstring / Quads / Groin

Slowly lower head to straight leg . . . Pause and roll back
to lying position . . . Return and repeat to other side.

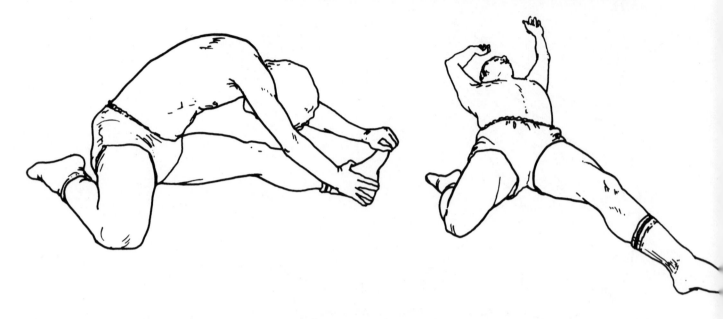

Groin

Tuck position . . . Lower knees to ground . . . Pause and
return. . . . Perform exercise using one leg at a time
before using both.

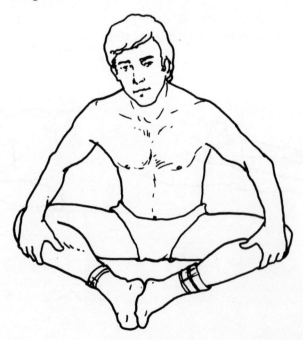

Hamstring / Groin

Lower head to knee . . . Use wide straddle . . . Pause and return . . . Repeat to other side. . . . Keep both legs locked.

Groin / Hamstring

Perform hurdler's stretch . . . Pause . . . Return to other side.

3 Equipment

Equipment that fits properly will make you look like a football player, but more important, provides the best possible protection. Serious injury may result from ill-fitting equipment, and a quarterback can't lead a team if he's injured.

Athletic Supporter

Protection of the groin region is important. The athletic supporter provides the necessary protection. If the supporter should move out of place you will be uncomfortable and can be injured. So always make sure the supporter straps are in good shape. The cup should offer complete protection. Using a clean and dry supporter is very important; if it is wet or damp, you may develop an uncomfortable and unsanitary rash.

Underwear

Weather conditions at game time determine the amount of underwear worn. Under normal conditions, the necessary underwear should include a T-shirt, which will absorb the sweat and protect against shoulder pads rubbing the skin; and a pair of gym shorts, which, when worn under the athletic supporter, gives added padding under the hip pads, helps to absorb the sweat, and protects from injury and infection.

Knee Pads

The knee pads are designed to protect you from damage due to falls and scrapes and should extend below and above the kneecap to protect the muscles and cartilage adjacent to the knee. Some players cut their pads to cover just their kneecaps, sacrificing protection for speed. I feel you can be just as fast, and have good protection, by not cutting down your pads.

The first time pads are worn they seem cumbersome and uncomfortable. However, once you have begun playing, the discomfort of the pads is quickly forgotten.

Thigh Pads

Thigh pads are designed to fit around the front of your leg and absorb the shock of being tackled. They should cover the front of the thigh, almost touching the top of the knee pads. The amount of area covered by the pads depends on the size of your thigh.

The tops of thigh pads are cut on an angle, running from the inside of your legs outward at about 45 degrees. The reason for the angle is to provide the best possible protection while allowing you to run without pinching in the groin region.

The combination of knee and thigh pads will protect the front of the leg from just below the knee to the top of the thigh. The pads are light in weight and durable. Their purpose is to protect you from injury and not hinder your performance. Remember, though, that pads offer only some protection; your chances of avoiding serious injury are greatly increased if you keep your legs in good shape.

Pants

Today most pants are made of stretch material, so that they fit snugly and hold your pads in place. On the inside of the pants are four pockets, two holding the thigh pads and two holding the knee pads, preventing them from slipping out of proper position. A well-fitting pair of pants not only adds protection to your legs and hips, but also gives a neat appearance.

Hip Pads

There are two types of hip pad: a strap-on type and a girdle type. The strap-on type resembles an old Western gun belt with two holsters and has a piece of plastic attached to the back to protect the end of your spine.

The girdle-type pads fit in a pant fashion. The pads in the girdle are fitted into the stretch material at the hip and a piece is inserted to protect the end of the spine; whereas the strap-on type has the pads on the outside, the girdle type has the pads inserted into inside pockets. There is also a slight difference in the way each is put on. Strap-on pads are strapped on; you step into girdle pads as you would a pair of shorts. There are also hip pads that are larger at the top to protect your lower back and kidneys.

The type of hip pads you choose to wear are simply a matter of personal comfort; both kinds provide protection. I prefer the girdle type; they fit me more comfortably than the strap-on and seem to stay in place better.

When putting on hip pads, make sure the pads completely cover your hips and the end of your spine. Remember, a quarterback can never have too much protection.

Wrist Bands

Some quarterbacks prefer to tape their wrists to stop sweat from rolling onto their hands, but I prefer using wrist bands (tennis bands). They are made of cloth and allow full movement of the wrist as well as stopping perspiration from rolling onto the hands. Sweat on your hands makes handling the ball difficult.

There are special types of wrist bands that allow you to write plays on them for reference during the course of a game. These wrist bands, called *cheaters,* must be specially ordered. The cloth bands are relatively inexpensive and can be bought in most sports stores.

Shoulder Pads

The shoulder pads protect the shoulders, collar bone, and chest bone.

There are different sizes of shoulder pads. The smallest ones are used generally by quarterbacks and receivers, the larger ones by linemen and backs. Both sizes protect the same areas and with the same efficiency.

If your pads are too small, they will fit too tightly and pinch around the neck. If they are too loose, they won't protect you adequately. When trying on pads, be sure they fit securely and do not interfere with your throwing motion.

When you put on your pads, adjust the straps so they aren't twisted. Check both sets of laces, front and back, to see that they are not frayed. If you are hit, frayed laces could break causing you either injury or a couple of missed plays. Be sure the actual shoulder pads extend to cover your shoulders completely. The pads should come just to the tops of your biceps.

If your shoulder pads fit poorly you can be hurt seriously and ruin your career as a quarterback.

Helmets

There are several types of helmet: air-filled, liquid-filled, completely padded, and suspension, as well as combinations of these. I have tried all of them and have been happy with the protection they have given me.

The importance of complete head protection has led to more research aimed at improving the durability and safety of helmets than any other piece of football equipment.

Helmet sizes vary according to the size of the head. Make sure the helmet you choose fits properly. If it is too tight, it can cause headaches; too loose, and it can result in a broken nose. The helmet should feel snug when you first put it on; sweating tends to loosen the helmet and make it more comfortable. So don't decide on a helmet just because it fits well when you first try it. Choose one that's a little snug, work up a sweat, then decide whether it fits properly.

Unobstructed vision is important to a quarterback. The helmet should not in any way obstruct the field of vision. When trying on a helmet be aware of not only your forward, but also *peripheral* vision—what you can see out of the corner of your eye. With your head at a forward position, you should be able to see clearly to both sides.

The choice of a face mask depends entirely on the individual. When choosing your face mask, be sure it protects and allows clear vision. An ill-placed face mask may also obstruct vision; for this reason be aware of its position.

There are many different kinds of face masks. The most conventional is a double bar, but masks vary from single bars to full cages. The purpose of bars is to protect the face from injury. I prefer to wear a single bar worn at a

Keep the ball up while looking downfield.

Photo by Dick Darcy, *Washington Post*

sloping angle, as it allows me complete vision and adequately protects my face.

Not all people wear the same hat size or like the same style. This same principle applies to your helmet and face mask. Be sure to get the proper fit and protection. You only get one head, so take care of it.

Shoes

Next to your helmet, the shoes are probably the most important piece of equipment. If your feet are bothering you in any way your performance will be affected. If shoes are too big you will feel sloppy moving in them; if they're too tight you'll get blisters, which can result in even more serious problems.

When buying shoes, be aware of the quality of material they are made of. Shoes made of leather or kangaroo should be a bit snug at first as they will stretch to your foot size. Shoes made of other materials normally will not stretch; consequently, buy all non-leather shoes in a comfortable fit. Remember to take along or wear a pair of socks similar to the ones you will wear when using the shoes.

Shoe soles must differ to conform to the different types of playing surfaces. The conventional football shoe has about seven cleats, five on the front of the sole and two on the heel. Most cleats are about three-eighths of an inch long and work well on grass fields. They can either be screwed into the sole (male cleats) or the cleat must be screwed onto a rod extending out from the sole (female cleats). The other type of sole is usually made of some kind of rubber or plastic with any number of cleats.

There are also different kinds of "turf" shoes. The best of these should keep slipping at a minimum and should not get too hot when worn for a couple of hours on artificial turf. A heat-resistant sole is extremely important for comfort, as it is usually fifteen degrees warmer on artificial turf than on grass. Football shoes should fit comfortably and offer support in the toes and arches.

Lacing the shoes properly is very important. To avoid pinching in the instep when you run, pull the laces together evenly. A trick I learned in lacing shoes is not to pull them too tightly when you first put them on. Like the rest of your body, your feet have to loosen up; after you have had your shoes on for a while, adjust your laces more tightly. Now you're ready to run like the wind.

Before putting on your shoes, cut your toenails to be even with your toes; you'll find it's more comfortable when you're cutting and pivoting. If you have a blister or cut on your foot, give it immediate attention. Early care of such foot problems can avoid a more serious and irritating problem later.

Elbow Pads

Today many more teams are playing on artificial turf. The elbow pads protect the elbows when you fall and also add some extra protection to the arm when you get hit.

I just wear one on my left arm. I have a superstition about wearing things on my throwing arm—I won't wear anything. However, elbow pads do add extra protection and are, again, an individual's preference.

The type of elbow pad I use is called a Helbow. It fits like a sock over the elbow and has a pad to protect the elbow area. It is light and gives me maximum protection.

How To Care for Your Equipment

In order to last, equipment must have proper care. Time spent on keeping your equipment in good condition is well worth the effort.

Some of the pieces of equipment may seem a bit costly, but the extra cost should be considered an investment, for you are getting good-quality material that will last.

Shoes

Are your cleats worn down? They should not be if you haven't been walking on asphalt or concrete. When traveling to practice or games, carry your shoes until you get to the field to help keep the cleats in good condition.

Are any cleats missing?

Are your laces still good?

Is the shoe cracked or torn? Cracking usually occurs after playing in mud or on wet turf. Place your shoes in an area where they can dry naturally; don't put them by a furnace or heater.

Shoulder Pads

Are the laces still good?

Are any of the straps broken?

Are all the plastic pieces in place?

Are all the rivets in place?

Athletic Supporter

Are all the straps secure? Check especially around the waist and cup.

Is the cup shabby? Be sure there aren't any tears or shredding in the cup.

Is the elastic around the waist still tight enough? After many washings the elastic around your waist will stretch. For better protection and fit, change to a new supporter.

Pants

Is the belt broken? If so, get a new one.

Are the pockets for the pads torn? If the pockets are torn, get a new pair of pants. The pads could slip when you are playing and you could be seriously hurt.

Is the elastic around the knee stretched out? The knee pads are held up by this elastic. To keep the pads in place you should be sure the elastic isn't broken or stretched.

Hip Pads

If you are using the strap-on type of hip pads, check for cracking in the belt. If there are cracks, get a new set of pads; the belt might break while you are playing and the pads will slip leaving your hips and tail bone unprotected.

If you are wearing girdle pads, be sure the pockets for the pads aren't torn.

Check the elastic in the waist and legs.

Hang pads up after using them so they can dry before the next practice.

Thigh Pads

Is the plastic insert broken? If so, get some new ones. Is the rubber covering cracked? You can fix this by taping the crack.

Helmet and Face Mask

Is the chin strap in good condition? Check to see if the straps are cracking; if so, get a new helmet.

Are the snaps tight? The snaps fastening the chin strap to the helmet can be tightened with a screwdriver.

Is the suspension tight?

Are all the pads snapped into place?

Is the face mask cracked or bent? If it is, replace it.

Are the rivets holding the face mask secure?

Is the helmet cracked? When you are not using your helmet hang it up. When you aren't playing keep your helmet either in your hand or on your head; don't throw the helmet around.

If the equipment you are using is the property of your team or school, tell the team manager if there are any problems. He will fix them. If you own your equipment and something needs fixing, don't wait for someone else to fix it for you. Take care of your equipment—it makes the difference between getting hurt and staying healthy.

Packing Equipment

When packing your equipment to travel, place each piece carefully in the travel bag, making sure you have every piece. If you treat your equipment roughly when you pack, you could very easily break or lose something. Negligence in packing equipment can hurt you.

I always pack my bag the same way each time. This repetition of packing serves two purposes: it is a check to see if I have all of my equipment, and I am sure nothing will be damaged when it is shipped.

The first thing to go into the bag is my helmet. Then the shoulder pads go on top of it. I usually take two pair of shoes with me, placed at either end of the bag.

The knee and thigh pads are usually very durable, so I put them on top of the shoulder pads. I wear girdle hip pads, which can be folded together and fit between the shoulder pads and shoes. The remaining pieces of equipment—underwear, wrist bands, etc., fit between the shoulder pads and other pair of shoes. Before I zip up the bag, I look through my locker to be sure I haven't forgotten anything. That last look is very important—I almost forgot my pants and jersey! They can be folded neatly and placed right on top of the knee and thigh pads. I zip up the bag and now my equipment is ready to be shipped and I'm ready for another trip.

4 How To Play Quarterback

There are no deep, dark secrets to the art of playing quarterback. Almost anyone can learn the basic physical skills. The hard part comes when you start making decisions: which play to call, who to throw to, when to throw, and, probably the toughest task, reading defenses. It is this ability to dissect and analyze opposing defenses that makes a quarterback great.

No two quarterbacks play their position alike, but there are a number of basics that we all must follow. This book describes my playing style.

Calling the Play

Playing football, it has been said, is 85 percent mental and 15 percent physical. Playing quarterback is 90 percent mental and 10 percent physical.

Before you take your position behind the center, you should have first called a play in the huddle. The play must be carefully selected. Your decision is based on the down and distance, weather conditions, field position, the time remaining on the clock, and the score.

Photo by Nate Fine

Take your position in the huddle and keep your head up.

The *down and distance* determine whether you will pass or run. Usually you run on first down, possibly on the second. If you have more than eight yards on any down it is wise to try a pass, screen, or possibly a draw.

If the *weather* is rainy or snowy, try to establish your running game. Running the football is the best way to control the ball and make the fewest mistakes.

When you *have the ball in your own end,* don't be careless. The area inside the twenty-yard line is called the "four-down" area. This means you should be able to get the ball into position so you can either punt or establish some kind of drive to keep the opposing team from getting the ball deep in your end. Going in on their twenty, you should be able to get *some* points, either a field goal or touchdown, in four downs.

The *time remaining on the clock and the score* determine whether you have to run or pass. If you have a substantial lead, it's best to keep the ball on the ground. If you are losing and time is running out, you must try to score in the quickest way possible—by passing. If the score is close, you will certainly have discussed a plan with your coach. When I'm in a game with the score close and time running out, I use the plays that have been most successful during the game. It's most important in this situation that you keep control of the ball.

Before the game even begins, you should prepare for any possible situation by studying films and meeting frequently with your coaches.

After you have selected the right play, break the huddle and hustle to the line of scrimmage. *Be a leader.*

Position in the Huddle

Some coaches like their quarterbacks to kneel down in the center or to the side of the huddle. Others want the quarterback standing at the back. Where the quarterback lines up is decided by the coach. No matter where he is, when he calls the play his voice should be just loud enough to be heard by everyone in the huddle and soft enough that it doesn't carry to the defensive players.

The Stance

It is important when you take your stance that you don't give away the play. The best way to avoid this is by assuming the same stance for runs and passes, going either right or left.

Your stance should be as natural as possible. Your feet are parallel and spread about the width of your shoulders. Your weight should be equally distributed, but slightly toward your toes. Your knees should be bent only slightly. Your hands should be placed under the center's crotch, with the back of your right wrist pressing firmly against the center's butt.

If you are right-handed, your right hand goes on top. If you are left-handed, your left does. The exact position of your hands depends on what's comfortable for you and the size of your center. With a tall center you won't have to put your hands in as deep as you would with a smaller center.

Your hands are joined at the thumbs with the right palm facing the ground and the left palm facing forward. The left hand is used as a stopper in case the center brings the snap up low. Your fingers should be spread and relaxed at all times, your elbows slightly flexed.

When calling signals, it is very important that you stand tall so you can see the defense clearly. Look to both sides before calling a play. First check to see that your team is set; then study the defense to determine whether you should call an audible.

Photo by Dick Darcy, *Washington Post*

Setting up with the proper stance.

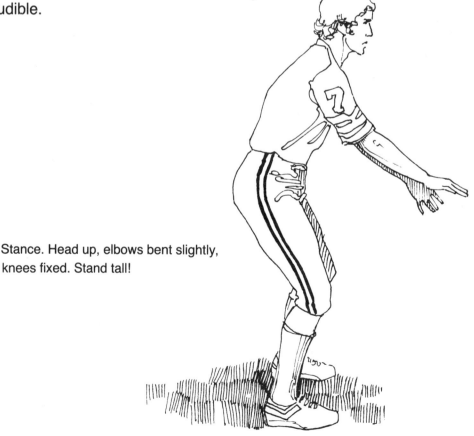

Stance. Head up, elbows bent slightly, knees fixed. Stand tall!

Audibles

Audibles are plays called at the line of scrimmage instead of in the huddle. They allow for last-minute changes against the present defensive alignment. When a quarterback calls a play in the huddle, he is faced with the possibility that the play he has called will be a poor selection. If the play you called is a poor choice, select another one. The most common audibles are quick passes or quick-hitting running plays.

You have only a few seconds to choose another play. You must be sure of the play you have picked; don't just grasp at straws.

In calling audibles most teams use a "live" color or number. The color or number said at the beginning of the cadence alerts your teammates that an audible is going to be called. The next number called is your audible. For example, let's say that a play is called on two and the live color is red. The quarterback gets into his stance, then says, "RED 42, set—hut one hut two." The center snaps the ball on the second "hut" and the team executes play 42. Because many teams have different ways of calling a play, the number 42 can mean one thing to one team and something different to another.

If a team is well-prepared for a game, the quarterback will probably only call about five or six audibles in a game. On the other hand, if the opposing team is playing entirely differently than was expected, the quarterback could call as many as thirty to thirty-five audibles.

How To Read Defenses

Reading defenses is probably the most difficult job for a quarterback. If you can master this aspect of the game, you will be a more complete and successful quarterback.

When reading a defense you are looking for either one-on-one coverage or trying to get a receiver in one of the voided areas of the zone coverage. But, before you begin to try to read defenses you should first understand the five basic types:

1. Man-to-Man

2. Strong Zone

3. Combination Coverage

4. Double Zone

5. Weak Zone

Once you understand the strengths and weaknesses of each defense they will be easier to read and attack.

When studying a team's defense you will see that each individual team has its own style. This will be pointed out to you by scouts, by your coach, and through film study. These tendencies are such things as what a team plays on first or second down, whom they substitute on passing downs and whether they prefer to play man-to-man, zones, or combination coverage.

There are four basic principles to reading defenses and executing pass plays against them:

Pre-read the coverage. You "pre-read" a defense when you set your team at the line of scrimmage just prior to taking the snap. This will give you an indication of the type of coverage a team is going to play.

One thing to look for is the "depth" of the cornerbacks and safeties. If they appear to be playing back there is a good chance the coverage will be some type of a zone. If the cornerbacks and safeties are *looking at the receivers* and playing about five to seven yards deep, you are probably going to get some type of man to man or combination coverage.

Key the proper defensive people. To "key" on a player means to watch him, particularly to see what assignment or location he appears to be heading for as soon as the ball is snapped.

Defenses are coordinated. Where any one player goes will usually tell you where the others will be going. This allows you to "key" or read a particular player and thus have a good grasp of what is happening with the rest of the defensive coverage.

You should start to key the defense *on your first two steps.*

Which player you key will depend on the type of pass pattern you are running. For example, if you are throwing a pass to your tight end or your wide receiver, you'll want to key one of the safeties. If you are throwing to a back, you should key a linebacker.

Work the pass pattern out. Once you have picked the *side* of the defense you want to work, think through the pattern you intend to run against that defense. As the play unfolds, give first consideration to the deepest pass route. If a completion there seems doubtful, work down toward the shorter routes—ending with the ones usually run by your backs. Keep in mind that most pass patterns are called with a particular down and a particular distance in mind. If, for example, what you need at the moment is a sure first down, the longest route should probably *not* be considered first.

Make a good decision. This is the most important part of reading a defense and executing a pass pattern. You should always try to choose the receiver with the best chance for a completion—depending upon the needed yardage or score.

Don't think you can beat every defense. If you don't have a receiver open, don't force a throw. Instead, throw the ball away. Remember, you have eleven guys trying to execute a play and they have eleven guys trying to stop you. Every now and then they will.

Reading the defense

Exactly how you read a defense depends upon the type of pass pattern being run. We'll take a look at two specific routes. One is a good first-and-ten or second-and-seven pass called the "Double Sponge." The other is a pass designed for third-and-short—the "Halfback Option."

The "Double Sponge" is very common to most levels of football, and you may have another term for it. On this particular pass the tight end and the flanker go to the same side and the split end goes to the opposite side. The backs line up in what we call a split back position:

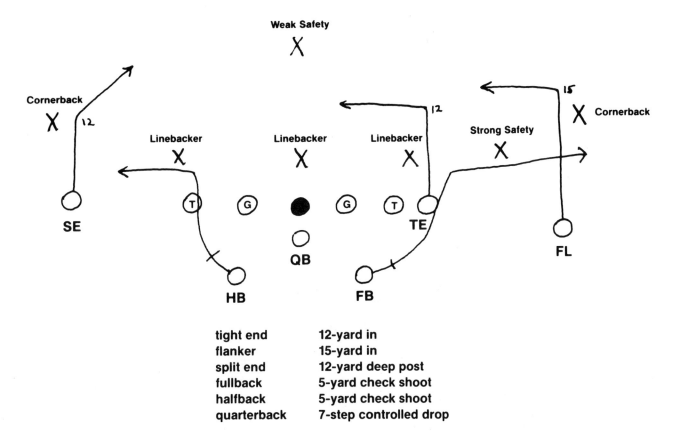

tight end	12-yard in
flanker	15-yard in
split end	12-yard deep post
fullback	5-yard check shoot
halfback	5-yard check shoot
quarterback	7-step controlled drop

The man to key in this play is the weak safety. If he moves toward the deep middle to cover the split end, you should work toward the tight end side or "strong" side. This decision can be made on your first two steps.

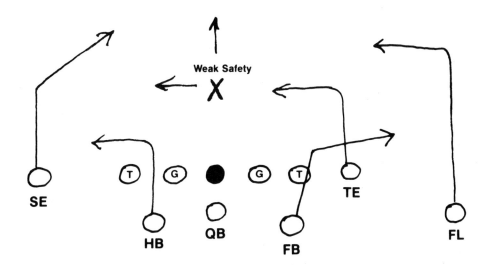

Once you have chosen the side to work, try to get the ball to the tight end. If he is covered, work out toward the flanker. If you don't think he is open, work down to the back or throw the ball away.

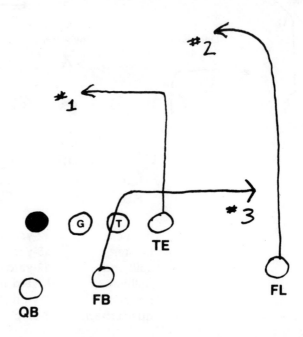

If the weak safety moves toward the strong side or up to cover the tight end, you'll have your chance to go for the big score to the split end. This is the best situation a quarterback can hope for—one-on-one.

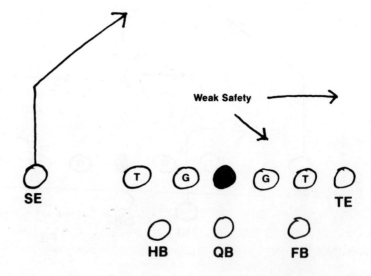

Keep in mind that this pass route is usually called in longer yardage situations when you are expecting a zone defense. But, you still have to take your proper key in case the defense changes up.

The next pass we will look at is used in shorter yardage situations—usually on third down. It is simply called the "Halfback Option." The halfback is your primary receiver, and you'll be keying the linebackers as they drop back. All your receivers must run their designated routes.

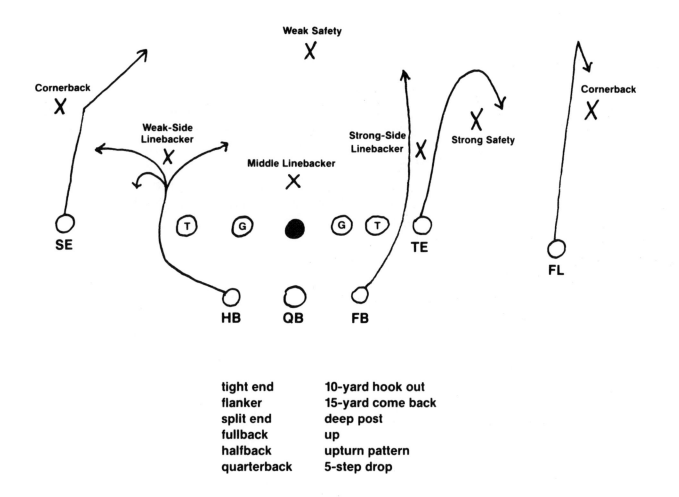

tight end	10-yard hook out
flanker	15-yard come back
split end	deep post
fullback	up
halfback	upturn pattern
quarterback	5-step drop

If the middle linebacker drops back and the weak-side linebacker runs to take away the short zone, the back will probably sit down in the voided area between them.

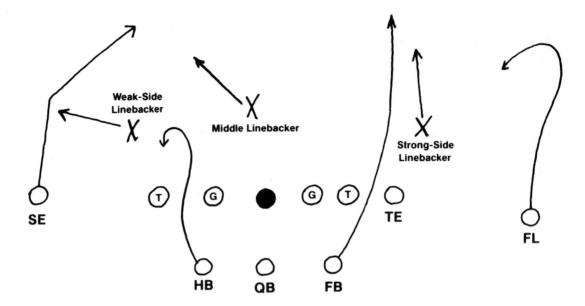

If the middle linebacker moves to cover the fullback going up the field and the weak-side linebacker is eyeing the halfback, he is probably covering him man-to-man. As I mentioned earlier, this is the best possible situation. The back now has the option of beating the linebacker inside or outside. If you can hit your back on the break, he could turn a five yard pass into a fifty-yard completion.

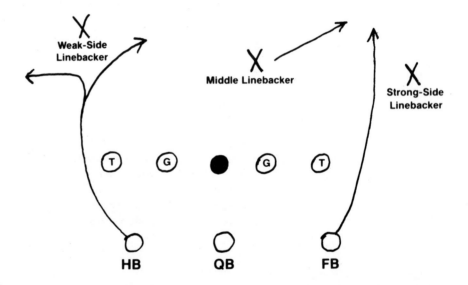

There are two things to keep in mind when throwing to a back. Deliver the ball on time and keep your throw close to his body. If you are late or your back has to reach or jump to catch the ball, you could put him in a position to get killed.

Reading defenses may not sound very difficult when you have a chance to sit down and read about it. The tough part is trying to keep up with the constant changes that are being made during actual play. You have to make all your decisions in the space of about 2.5 seconds.

This method of reading defenses should give you a good foundation to build on. After all, these principles helped me to quarterback the Redskins to the NFL World Championship in 1982.

Much of what I have told you so far is what to do. Now I'm going to give you a few things *not* to do:

1. Don't try to force the ball to a covered receiver. You'll probably wind up with an interception.

2. Don't take too few steps when dropping back. You will be ready to throw before your receivers have finished running their patterns.

3. Don't take too many steps when dropping back. Your throw will be late.

4. Don't hold the ball too long in the pocket. This will get you sacked.

5. Don't throw back into the middle of the field after sprinting out. The middle is where everyone is coming from to get you.

6. Don't try to look off a defensive back too long. You'll forget about your receivers.

The Exchange

This is where every play starts. A mistake here and you'll never run a play. The center and quarterback must both execute their jobs perfectly, or a fumble will result. The quicker the exchange is made, the faster the play can be executed.

1. The quarterback's top hand is pressed firmly against the center's butt in order to give the center a target for the ball.

2. The center brings up the ball, with a one-quarter turn, as quickly as possible.

3. The ball hits the quarterback's hand with the laces on the fingertips of the top hand.

4. As the ball hits the top hand with a "pop," the bottom hand closes on the ball.

5. When receiving the ball, the quarterback rides the center out of his stance to ensure a clean exchange. This is done by riding the arms forward with the movement of the center.

6. After the quarterback receives the ball, he immediately brings it to his stomach, parallel to the ground. A quarterback refers to his stomach as his third hand. Whether handing off, faking, or passing, always bring the ball to your stomach after taking the snap. This prevents a pulling guard from knocking the ball from your hands and ensures a clean exchange from center.

Pivots Used by a Quarterback on Running Plays

Front Pivot

The most natural pivot for a quarterback to perform is used for quick-hitting and dive plays.

1. After taking the snap from center, bring the ball to your stomach, keeping your elbows close to your body.

2. Take a short step, about one foot, with your lead foot down the line of scrimmage. If you are going right, your lead foot is the right foot. At the same time you are taking your lead step, your head should be turned and looking for the halfback.

3. As you cross your leg over for the second step, shift your weight to your right foot as you extend your arms to the halfback's stomach. Try to be as close to the back as possible in order to ensure a clean hand-off. Staying close to the ball carrier will help in your faking.

Getting ready to take the snap.

Sweep Pivot

The name tells you the type of play on which you use this pivot.

1. After taking the snap from center, bring the ball to your stomach, keeping your elbows close to your body. (We will assume that you are handing off to start a sweep to the left.)

2. Bring your right leg straight back as far as you can, slightly pivoting on your left foot. At the time you take your first step, turn your head to look for the ball carrier.

3. Take your second step in about a 30-degree angle to the ball carrier; you step toward the back to allow him clear vision of the blocking ahead of him. Also, the sooner the halfback gets the ball, the better his opportunity to make his move.

When you hand-off, remember to extend your arms and shift your weight toward the ball carrier.

Reverse Pivot

This pivot is used mostly on off-tackle plays and run-action pass plays; instead of the quarterback opening toward the back, he opens away from him. Let's assume we are running an off-tackle play to the left.

1. While taking the snap, your hands will ride the center forward. Your body will be moving backward.

Carrying out my fake after a hand-off.

Photo by Nate Fine

2. Bring your right leg as far back as you can, to about a 120-degree angle. While making this first move, bring the ball to your stomach. Keep your elbows close to your body to conceal the ball from the defense.

3. When you take your second step, pivot on your right toe, bringing your left leg across. At the same time, turn your head and locate the halfback.

4. Again shift your weight from your right leg to your left.

5. Extend your arms forward to hand the ball off.

   As I am sure you notice, most pivots only differ at the start and are basically the same during the hand-off.

Making a Proper Hand-Off

1. Keep both hands on the football until you actually hand off.

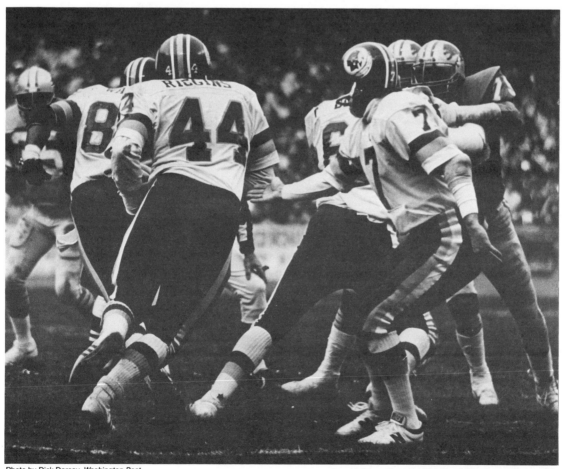

Photo by Dick Darcey, *Washington Post*

Looking the ball in while handing off.

2. At the time you hand the ball off, release the hand closest to the back. Lay the ball in flat, forward of your vision, not behind it, and as nearly horizontal as possible. It should go in with a slight force and cause a light thud on contact in the stomach area.

3. Immediately, the ball carrier feels for a point of the ball with the webbing of his fingers and eases it to one side.

4. Follow through on the hand-off by letting the hand holding the ball slide off it as the back moves toward the hole.

Faking a Hand-Off

Faking is very important to the success of a play. A good fake by the quarterback can often cause one or more defensive players to take a few steps in the wrong direction.

When faking a hand-off to a back, get as close as possible to him. In most instances you should stick the ball into the faking back's stomach, always keeping both hands on the ball. Although a defensive player may see you stick the ball into a back's stomach, the blocking patterns may cause him to lose sight of the play for just a moment. When the defensive player's vision is blocked, he must pause, just for a second, to see if the hand-off was actually made or not.

The other half of a good fake must come from the back. It is always a good policy to have the back run as naturally as possible while faking; then the defense can't be sure whether or not he has the ball.

Faking a Pass

1. Fake with your eyes. When setting up to throw, look in the direction opposite to the way you intend to throw. This will keep the defense guessing. Many defensive backs read a quarterback's eyes, figuring that a quarterback looks where the ball is going. It isn't necessarily so. There is a natural tendency for someone to relax when he isn't being watched. You can get this feeling in team meetings or in a classroom; if the coach or instructor is looking at you, you'll look right at him and

listen intently. If he looks to the other side of the room, you'll feel a bit more relaxed. The same thing applies to defensive backs—if you look at them they'll be ready and react quickly to your throw. If you look away they'll relax a little and can be beaten much more easily.

2. Pump your arm. Defensive backs are taught to keep one eye on the receiver and the other eye on the quarterback. As soon as a deep back sees the quarterback start his throwing motion he begins to react in the direction he thinks the ball is going. So when you pump your arm, follow through with the ball. Many touchdowns have been scored by quarterbacks who had actually started to throw to a receiver, then, at the last minute, hung onto the ball. We call this "reloading." By the time the defensive back has committed himself in the wrong direction, the receiver runs by him for a touchdown.

It takes time to learn how to fake well. Whether you are faking a hand-off, faking with your eyes, or pump-faking a pass, take the time to make it look like the real thing. You and your coach will be pleased with the results.

Plays in which a Quarterback Carries the Ball

There are very few plays in an offense designed for the quarterback to carry the football. Two that do appear in every offense are the quarterback sneak and the quarterback draw.

Quarterback Sneak

This play is used to gain short yardage, usually no more than a yard. In our club, if there is less than a yard to go for a first down, the policy is that the quarterback should sneak for it. Usually just by falling forward you can gain a yard.

Sometimes it gets a little more difficult than just falling forward. The line forms a wedge around the center and fires out, cutting off the charge of the defensive line. Just stay as close to the center as possible. Put your head down and keep both hands on the ball, and you'll usually get the necessary yardage.

Keeping the ball close while scrambling.

Photo by Dick Darcey, *Washington Post*

Quarterback Draw

This is more of a surprise play and is used only once or twice in a game. The quarterback draw serves the same purpose as a screen or halfback draw; it is used to slow down a pass rush, especially if you are being pressed by the defensive ends. The play starts out looking like a drop-back pass. The better an actor you are the more successful the play will be—you must make it look like a pass, so that the linebackers will start their drops and your linemen will have a chance to steer the on-rushing linemen to an outside rush.

1. Take the snap from center and drop back two or three steps.

2. When you reach a depth of about three or four yards, plant your right foot and push off forward.

3. Tuck the ball under your arm and run to the open area.

This play will not only slow down the rush but can also break for a touchdown and change the tempo of a game.

The Passing Game

To be a complete quarterback you must be able to throw a football. You have to know when to throw, who to throw to, and how to throw. Becoming a good passer doesn't happen overnight; hours of hard work and sacrifice go into it.

Passing is an art. Like any artist, you, the quarterback, must develop your own style. There is no right or wrong way to throw a football, but there are certain guides we all should follow.

Every play, whether it's running or passing, should look the same at the beginning. Only after the exchange is made do the plays start to vary. If you can keep the defense guessing on every play, it will be to your advantage.

Pivots Used in a Passing Game

Drop-Back (Pocket) Pivot

The drop-back pass is the backbone of any team's passing game. When dropping back to pass there are two ways to pivot:

Dropping back sideways. This is the most common way to pivot.

1. Shift your weight slightly to your left foot just before the ball is snapped, then kick your right leg back as far as possible. This motion can start a half cadence before the ball is snapped.

2. When the ball is snapped, ride the center's butt forward to ensure a good exchange.

3. After you receive the ball, bring it to your stomach, then pivot and push off the ball of your left foot. This whole motion should take no more than three-tenths of a second.

Backpedaling. There really isn't an actual pivot when you backpedal to pocket, although the basics are very similar to the sideways move. Shift your weight before the snap, ride the center's butt forward for a good exchange, then push off with the toe of your foot and begin to pocket. Which foot you choose to lead with is up to you.

A common mistake when dropping back is to take a false step—taking a step forward before dropping your foot back to pass can cost you half a second. To avoid taking a false step, shift your weight slightly to your left foot, if you kick back with your right, just before the ball is snapped. This will cause your left foot to stay planted so you can turn and pivot without false-stepping and losing time.

Wasted steps affect the entire timing of the play.

Sprint-Out Pivot

The sprint-out pivot is very similar, in many respects, to the sideway pocket pivot, the basic difference being the angle at which you kick your leg back. If you are going to the right, kick your right leg back at about a 60-degree angle, then pivot and push off your left foot. If you are going to the left, kick your left leg back.

Delivering under pressure.

Photo by Dick Darcey, *Washington Post*

The shifting of your weight to avoid false-stepping is very important. If you are a step slow, your vision may be blocked by the penetration of the defensive end and disrupt the timing of the play. You can only expect your offensive line to block for so long, so don't be late.

Run-Action Pivots

The run-action pivots vary according to the plays called. Just as the name implies, the pivots are the same as those for the various running plays: front, sweep, and reverse.

Types of Passes

Drop-Back (Pocket) Pass

Most pass offenses are made up of about 75 percent drop-back passes, 15 percent sprint-out passes, and 10 per cent run-action passes. The drop-back pass is used most frequently because it is the easiest to teach and execute.

Drop-back passes are thrown from a "pocket" about seven yards behind the line of scrimmage. The pocket is an open but protected area, formed by the offensive linemen, in which the quarterback can stand to throw.

Dropping back is vitally important because it sets up the entire play. The quarterback must not only pocket quickly, but must also read the defense and decide which receiver he is going to throw to. I drop back sideways when throwing deep and backpedal when throwing short; I sometimes vary my drops to confuse the defense, but this is usually the pattern.

Drop-Back Sideways

1. Keep your eyes on the defensive secondary. Once you have taken the snap, pull the ball to your stomach, then up to your chest region in one smooth motion.

2. To pocket sideways, reach back with your right foot as far as you can, then scissor the left leg across and over the right.

When you pocket, your weight is on your right foot. After reaching the depth you want, plant your right foot,

Pocketing.

a. Good drop step . . .

b. Looking downfield . . .

Photo by Nate Fine

c. Ball up . . .

d. Plant . . .

e. Stop and shift weight . . .

f. Air under back heel . . .

then step forward on your left as you start your throwing motion. Shift your weight when throwing to give your passes more crispness and power.

I try to drop back ten to twelve yards. This is about three yards deeper than most quarterbacks, but I find it gives me a better view of the secondary and my receivers. All this should take about 1.5 seconds. By the time you reach the proper depth you should have chosen a receiver to throw to and still have about one second to release the ball.

Backpedaling

Backpedaling is a slower method than dropping back sideways. You simply back up as fast as you can, pushing off the balls of your feet until you reach the proper depth. I use the backpedaling method to throw shorter passes because it allows me a complete view of the defensive secondary as I pocket.

1. After taking the snap from center, go through the same smooth motion of bringing the ball up to your chest region.

2. As you are pocketing, look over the defense. When setting up to pass, bring yourself under control.

3. Plant with your right foot, if you are a righty.

4. As you start to pass, shift your weight to your left foot. If you are shifting your weight properly when you deliver the ball, the heel of your back leg or even your whole foot will be off the ground. Always step in the direction of the receiver. Your stride should be about 2½ to 3 feet long. Don't overstride; this brings the trajectory of the ball down.

5. When you are setting up to pass, your body should be facing almost completely sideways. Your left shoulder will be leading; when you throw, rotate your upper body to be parallel with your receiver.

Drop-back passes are actually broken down into three stages: the snap, getting back, and setting up. *The snap* is important because you must have the ball to start any play. *Getting back* to the pocket as quickly as possible will give you time to look over the defense. Bring yourself under control when *setting up.* If you are off-balance when you deliver the ball, the pass will be poorly thrown and more easily intercepted than a pass thrown properly.

Timing

Speed is not the important thing in drop-back passing. It's *timing.* There is no defense for a perfectly timed pass. When you are ready to deliver the ball, your receiver must be just completing his pattern. If you are ready too soon or he makes his cut too soon, the defense will have time to react.

I have found a method that should help improve the timing of your delivery with the cut of your receivers. Take the distance of the pattern and divide it by two. That is how many steps you should take when pocketing. For example, most sideline patterns are run at ten yards, so divide ten by two; you should take five steps back from the line of scrimmage, then plant and be ready to throw. You can apply this method to both types of drop-back passes.

As you are setting up to pass, stay agile on your feet. While you are looking for a receiver, bounce slightly to keep in constant motion in case you are forced to scramble out of the pocket. If you get hit while standing flat-footed, you could seriously hurt a knee, so stay loose.

Sprint-Out Passes

The quarterback opens up to the play side and is running to pass. The sprint-out pass is especially difficult for a defense to cope with. They are never quite sure whether the quarterback is going to run with the ball or throw it.

Unlike drop-back passing, the quarterback can see only half of the defensive secondary as he sprints out to pass. He can therefore take a bit longer in deciding when to release the ball and who to throw to.

In sprint-out passes you will be throwing while running to the left or right. Being right-handed, I find it more difficult throwing while moving to my left. Throwing going to the left is an unnatural motion for right-handers and requires that I get my upper body facing upfield when delivering the pass. To have any degree of accuracy, I must adhere very closely to this basic of sprint-out passing.

Looking downfield on a sprint out.

Photo by Dick Darcey, *Washington Post*

Some quarterbacks will sprint out, then come to a complete stop when they are ready to throw, giving the defense a chance to react to the initial movement and defeating the purpose of the play.

As you pull away from the center, look immediately at the linebacker. If he penetrates, you should have a direct passing lane to the short receiver. If the linebacker drops back to defend, continue with the ball challenging the line of scrimmage. The longer you can keep the defense guessing, the more time your receivers have to get open. If the defense has all the receivers well covered, tuck the ball away and run with it. They can't defend against both the run and pass.

When throwing a sprint-out pass you should be completely on balance. Many interceptions occur because the quarterback is forced to throw while off-balance, causing a weak pass.

It is important for you to keep the ball up so that you can release it quickly and accurately. Young quarterbacks tend to sprint out with the ball down around their belts. By the time they see a receiver open and get the ball up to throw, the defensive man has closed the distance on the receiver and is in a position to break up the play or intercept.

The position of your body has a great deal to do with throwing the ball on the run. On a drop-back pass, if you

Scrambling and looking for a receiver in Super Bowl XVII.

don't get yourself squared around the chances of completing the pass are still relatively good. If you throw on the run and don't get yourself squared around, the pass will probably be too high or too low, cutting down your chances of completion.

Throwing a sprint-out pass becomes much easier if you follow a few basic principles:

1. Always throw going toward the line of scrimmage with your shoulders square to the receiver, and follow through after your release. This is important when you are throwing in a direction unnatural to you—throwing to the left if you are a righty and vice versa.

2. Run toward the line of scrimmage as you prepare to release the football.

Photo by Nate Fine

Rotating my hips so my shoulders are facing up field while throwing on the run.

3. Keep the ball up so you don't waste time delivering the pass.

4. Rotate your hips so your shoulders are parallel to the receiver. If your hips and shoulders aren't turned upfield, the ball will go either over the receiver's head or into his feet. Delivering a pass off-balance and throwing across your body will cause the ball to be pulled down, and the pass will be thrown at the receiver's feet. By over-compensating, you wind up throwing the ball over the receiver's head. When you throw across your body, your hips and shoulders are facing the sideline, and you lose the power and accuracy you need to be a good sprint-out quarterback.

5. When releasing the ball, bring your elbow through first, then your wrist with a snap. Rotate your wrist in a counterclockwise direction and follow through.

6. After you release the ball, don't pull up. Keep moving forward toward the receiver as far as you can. The follow-through of your body is just as important as the follow-through of your arm.

A quarterback who can throw on the run, as well as from the pocket, poses a special problem to defenses. They must prepare for a number of different types of plays. If the defense stops your pocket passes, you can always loosen them up with sprint-out passes and run-action passes. The more things they have to try to stop, the less effective they will be.

Photo by Dick Darcey, *Washington Post*

Bringing the elbow through first, while delivering a pass.

Run-Action Passes

Run-action passes make up only about 10 percent of your pass offense, as they lose their effectiveness if you throw them too often. When executing a run-action pass, first fake a run, then set up to pass. Both you and the back must carry out your fakes. The more you can make the play look like a run, the better chance you will have of completing the pass.

After you receive the ball from center, proceed as if you were making a hand-off. One of the most frequently used run-action passes is an off-tackle play. With the ball brought into your stomach, make your reverse pivot just as you would for the running play. Keep the ball into your stomach and work from there. Before faking don't waste

Throwing on the run.

Photo by Nate Fine

time feeling for the laces, or you are likely to be in a poor position to give a proper fake. If the fake is poor, no one will be fooled and you will have defeated the purpose of the play.

When faking, extend your arms as far back as possible and stick the ball into the stomach of the running back. Ride him forward until your arms are fully extended toward the hole. The back must also be a good actor. After a good fake bring the ball up to the chest area, feeling for the laces. Then fight to get depth as you would when throwing a pocket pass, using either the sideways method or backpedaling, whichever is more comfortable.

By the time you are setting up to throw, your linemen will have formed their protection. The defense should have been fooled, so you can throw to predetermined receivers. Unlike drop-back or sprint-out passes, you don't have to read the defense from the snap of the ball. You can concentrate on your fake.

Photo by Nate Fine

Another way of throwing a run-action pass is to keep on the move after the fake. The most common faking action used is the sweep. This pass is thrown quickly and in the same manner as a sprint-out pass. Always remember to keep the ball up and face the receiver squarely when delivering the pass.

Where To Aim a Pass

Quite simply, throw the ball away from the defender. The exact spot to throw to depends on the position of the defensive back in relation to the receiver.

Curl-In Pattern

A curl-in pattern is where the receiver goes down about fifteen yards, plants his outside foot, then turns to the inside, creating an open lane between himself and the quarterback. Throw the ball belt-high so that the receiver can easily keep himself between the defensive player and the ball. If the defensive player is on the receiver's left, aim the ball to the right side. If the defender is on the right, aim the ball belt-high and to the left. If the pass were to end up at shoulder height, the defender could easily reach over and knock the ball down.

Side-Line Patterns

To run a side-line pattern to the right, the receiver goes down the proper distance, usually ten yards, plants his inside foot and squares out, looking for the ball over his inside shoulder. On sideline patterns to the right, I try to keep the ball at chest height, leading the receiver toward the sidelines by a step. This is the ideal position for a pass. If the defensive player has good position on the receiver, I'll throw the ball short and waist-high, forcing the receiver to come back for the ball so that he can gain a step on the defensive man covering him. In order to get the ball, the defensive man would have to come through the receiver and commit pass interference. Receivers usually prefer passes between the waist and shoulders. If you keep the ball in this area, your chances of completing passes are greatly increased.

Common Quarterback Errors

1. Twisting the wrist clockwise when releasing the ball. The pass is weak and flutters like a wounded duck in flight.

2. Rushing the fake on run-action passes. This is a bad mistake, because the fake becomes unconvincing and poorly executed. It won't fool the defense and therefore ruins the chances of a successful play.

3. Turning the head when pocketing, taking the eyes off the defense. This means you will have to waste time analyzing the defense when you set up to pass.

4. Throwing across the body when sprinting, causing short, weak passes.

5. Taking a false step while getting away from the line of scrimmage. Sloppy pivoting and time-consuming steps usually result from wasted steps.

6. Throwing while the weight is on the back foot. Throwing while off-balance means you must use all arm to throw, rather than your wrist. Often when a quarterback is being pressured the result is an off-balance pass.

5 The Game Plan

A game plan is put together by the coaching staff after hours of studying films looking for weaknesses and tendencies of the opposing defense. Are they a zone team or a man-to-man team? Which corner is weakest? Who do they substitute on long yardage situations? In short, the game plan is simply a "plan of attack" for taking on a specific team.

Joe Washington, Charlie Tayor and I talk strategy with Coach Gibbs.

Photo by Nate Fine

Keeping the ball high while delivering a pass.

The final plan will consist of a set of plays the coaches feel will have the greatest chance for success in certain situations. One category, for example, would be "first-and-ten situations." Some plays may be repeated in several categories. The plan will also include lists of plays to be used in certain areas of the field. In between the 40-yard lines, for example, is a favorite area for trick plays such as flea flickers, reverses, and any other plays the coaches may dream up late at night.

The most important of these areas is probably inside the 20-yard line. We call it the "RED AREA" or "plus-twenty." This is where the right decisions will put points on the board for your team. Those decisions will be based on such factors as time left, the score, and the defensive personnel. You never want to get to the "RED AREA" without a plan.

Things aren't always smiles.

When the coaches have finalized their game plan they will present it to the team. During those meetings you, as quarterback, must take good notes and ask questions. It's up to you to execute that plan. You must know it as well as the coaches by game time.

Hard work ahead of time will leave you with a game plan that should need little revision. The Boy Scouts say it best: "Be Prepared." Have a game plan you believe in, and stick with it.

6 The Two-Minute Offense

The two-minute offense is your way of taking advantage of the clock at the end of the half and the end of the ball game. It is usually saved for two specific situations: saving time on the clock if tied or behind, or wasting time on the clock if ahead during the final minutes of the game. Your ability to function smoothly and efficiently in these situations can have a great effect on the outcome of the game.

Knowledge of the rules as they apply to the game clock is the single most important factor in this phase of the game.

The wise use of your time-outs is the first factor to be considered. Each team is allowed three (3) time-outs per half. It is imperative you do not use any of your time-outs unnecessarily during the normal course of the game. If at all possible, you would like to have all three time-outs available for use in the two-minute offense.

Points To Remember During the Last Two Minutes

The Game clock *stops*:
- When time-out is called by the official
- On an incomplete pass
- When the ball carrier goes out of bounds
- During the administration of a penalty
- While the "chain gang" measures for a first down
- When the quarterback is tackled attempting to pass

The game clock *starts*:
- When the ball is legally touched on a kickoff
- With the snap of the ball:
  - After a called time-out
  - After an incomplete pass
  - After a ball carrier goes out of bounds
  - After the two-minute warning
  - After a kickoff out of the end zone that is not legally touched
  - After an exchange of possession

- After the administration of a penalty
- With the referee's whistle indicating ball ready for play:
  - After a measurement for first down
  - After an excess time-out
  - After a lateral out of bounds
  - After a "sack"

Quarterback's Guide for the Two-Minute Offense

Saving Time When Tied or Behind

1. You must be absolutely positive about the number of time-outs remaining.

2. Try not to use any of your time-outs until the final minute.

3. You must be certain that the team is aware of the fact that you are in the two-minute offense. Yell "Red Ball" loudly when it is apparent the clock will not be stopped. This will tell everyone to line up in the previous formation.

4. It is your responsibility to know all the rules regarding the stopping and starting of the game clock. You must be the absolute master of the situation.

5. The ball carriers must know whether you are thinking touchdown or field goal. They will fight harder for the long gainer when a touchdown is necessary. They will be more willing to run out of bounds in order to stop the clock if you are working for a field goal.

6. Recognize the situation in which you must intentionally throw the incomplete pass to stop the clock, or when you must go for the first down play to continue to control the ball.

7. Follow the game plan in calling plays that will allow the runner or receiver to get out of bounds if possible.

8. Follow the play closely and be prepared to line up and call a play at the line of scrimmage if you do not get the clock stopped. (Keep one eye on the bench for a visual signal from your coach.)

9. Request a measurement any time the ball is close to a first down.

10. Remember when it is necessary to have a play called, and have your team on the line of scrimmage, ready to go, as the referee signals the ball ready to play and starts the clock.

11. You must understand when a called time-out is necessary, and you must hustle to the closest official to get this time-out called quickly. You will call all time-outs unless the other designated player can expedite the time-out.

12. *Stay "cool" and remember: You are in charge.*

Wasting Time on the Clock When You Are Ahead

1. Use the full thirty seconds on each play whenever possible.

2. Keep the ball away from the sidelines.

3. Warn your runners and receivers to stay inbounds.

4. Remind your ball carriers to hold onto the ball and get up slowly.

5. If you have to kick, do not kick out of bounds or over the goal line.

6. Eliminate all penalties.

7. *Never* call a time-out.

8. If there are less than thirty seconds left on the clock, let the clock run without centering the ball.

7 How To Throw a Football

There's a lot more to throwing a football than meets the eye. You have to work diligently while learning to throw the ball correctly. If you develop poor throwing habits, it's difficult to correct them.

Grip

The first essential for distance and accuracy is a good grip. It's especially important in less-than-ideal weather conditions, when the ball becomes slippery.

Even if your hands are small, you can still develop a firm grip. There are many good passers with small hands; they have compensated by working that little bit extra on

a   b   c

a. Two hands on the ball. b. Keep ball high. c. Keep off-arm in, close to body. d. Shift weight. e. High release. f. Air under back heel, and follow through.

techniques. For instance, always keep both hands on the ball when setting up to throw and keep the ball close to your body until just before you start your throwing motion.

I find the best way to grip a football is with your fingers on the laces. Place your little finger just below the fourth lace and your middle finger at the top of the laces, with the laces resting just above the center joint of your middle finger.

The index and middle fingers, the last to leave the ball, are the ones that impart the spin. Your thumb is underneath the ball and should be about three inches down from the point.

Some quarterbacks grip a football with their palms resting on the ball. I prefer to use only my fingertips, keeping my palm off the ball. This allows a more secure grip and I find my delivery quicker and more accurate.

d   e   f

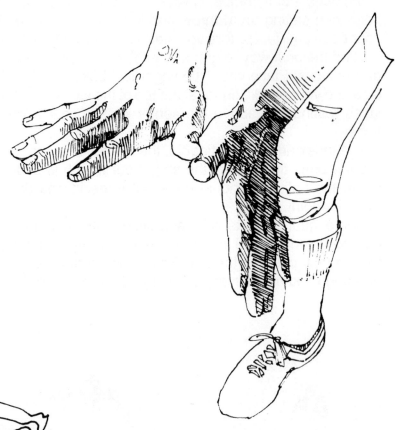

Gripping. Remember to keep fingers s-p-r-e-a-d.

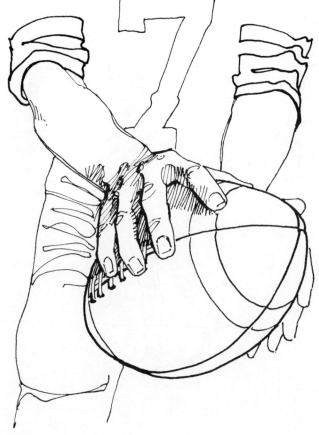

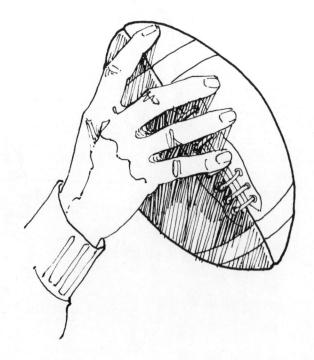

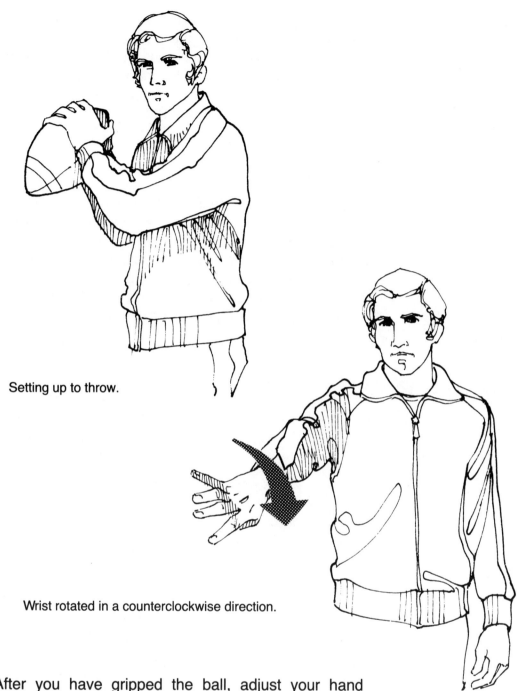

Setting up to throw.

Wrist rotated in a counterclockwise direction.

After you have gripped the ball, adjust your hand slightly until it feels comfortable. No two people have exactly the same hand size, so there will be slight variations between grips.

When setting up to throw, always keep both hands on the ball and keep the ball close to your shoulders until just before you start your throwing motion.

Now you're ready to throw. In many ways, throwing a football is similar to throwing a baseball. The major difference is that a pitcher rotates his wrist outward, or clockwise, whereas a quarterback rotates his in a counterclockwise direction. If the quarterback were to throw the way a pitcher does, the pass would be weak and the ball would wobble in flight. Furthermore, a quarterback's stride is much shorter; in stepping just two feet, he maintains good balance during delivery.

Release

At the time you release the ball, your shoulders should be square to your receiver. The release should be smooth and quick.

Bring the ball forward very close to your ear; if you keep the nose of the ball slightly tilted upward, the pass will be softer and easier to catch. Let your elbow lead the way, followed by a smooth, loose arm motion. Then snap your

Release. a. Keep ball up. b. Step toward receiver and rotate hips forward. c. Follow through.

wrist in a counterclockwise direction, so that when your follow-through motion is finished, your palm is facing the ground.

The most effective arm angle for delivering a pass is the three-quarter to overhand style. Choosing a style depends mainly on the individual; I prefer the three-quarter to overhand motion because it has been the most successful way to throw over the on-rushing linemen.

A good follow-through is important for distance and accuracy. After you release the ball, your hand should come across your body and your thumb should be pointing toward the ground.

Trajectory

The receiver gets the ball from the quarterback in one of two trajectories. The flat trajectory, in which the ball rarely gets more than eight to ten feet off the ground, is used to

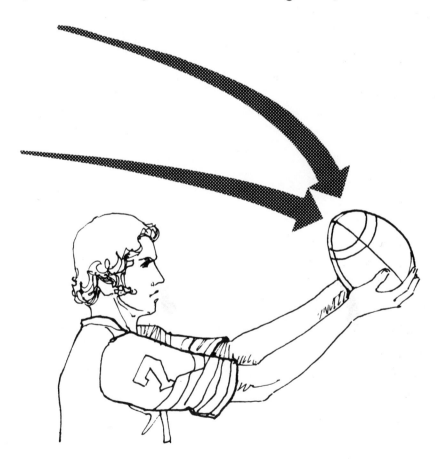

Trajectory.

throw the ball short distances. For deeper passes a loftier trajectory is recommended. By lofting the ball, you can get greater distance but you also increase your chances of interception.

When throwing a long pass, release the ball at a higher angle and with a greater extension of your throwing arm than you would use for short passes. To get the most power and distance from a pass, you need split-second timing between your step and release.

8 How To Hold for Extra Points and Field Goals

The kicking game has become a very important part of football over the past few years and is responsible for better than 15 percent of the points scored. The main reasons for the increase are the larger defensive linemen and the more complex defenses.

Players today are generally bigger and quicker than they were ten years ago. As a result, kickers must get more height on their kicks and speed up the time it takes to get them off.

Improved defenses make it more difficult for an offense to move the ball consistently; field goal attempts, therefore, must be made from further away.

The success of the place kicker usually depends on how good his holder is. If the ball isn't placed properly in about 1.9 seconds, the kick has a poor chance of getting off and less chance of being good.

How Deep Should the Holder be?

When holding, line up about seven yards directly behind the center. This distance gives you the best chance of getting the kick away. It is far enough back from the line of scrimmage so that the kick shouldn't be blocked by someone reaching up over the line of scrimmage. It is close enough to prevent the defensive men from rushing in from the outside and blocking the kick. They would have to come around your blockers to get to the ball instead of having a straight shot at it.

Position of the Holder

Kneel on one knee; if you are holding for a right-footed kicker, on your left, and on your right knee if holding for a lefty. Whether you are holding for a soccer-(side) style kicker or one that approaches the ball straight, your position should be about the same.

When kneeling, keep your front leg bent and point your toe toward the line of scrimmage. Rotate your upper body

Photo by Nate Fine

Winning field goal versus the Giants in overtime.

Photo by Dick Darcey, *Washington Post*

Keeping hand in place after ball has been kicked.

so you are facing the line of scrimmage. It is important you keep your front leg bent so that you can keep your balance in case you have to reach for a bad snap. It is also a form of protection. If a defensive player were to fall into you when your knee was locked, serious injury might result. When your knee is bent, you have more flexibility to roll with the hit.

Where Should the Ball be Spotted?

The kicker will mark where he wants the ball spotted. Most kickers will use tape, cloth, etc., to mark the spot, which will vary by about a yard depending upon your

Use just enough pressure to keep the ball in place.

Photo by Dick Darcey, *Washington Post*

position on the field. As you kneel, place your "down" knee parallel to the mark and about 12 inches from it. When you take your position, be sure you're not blocking either the follow-through or vision of the kicker.

After the kicker has marked the spot and taken his steps, assuming he is right-footed, place the forefinger of your left hand on the mark. This aids in putting the ball in the proper place after you receive the snap from center. While doing this, check that the kicker is ready. One of the most common errors made by holders is assuming the

Placing the ball. Mark where the ball should be spotted.

kicker is ready without asking him. To prevent this mistake, always turn directly toward the kicker and ask him if he is ready. As soon as he says "yes" or nods his head, turn and start the snap count. Don't keep the kicker waiting.

Where Should the Ball be Snapped?

The exact spot to which the ball is snapped depends on the holder's preference. Some like the ball snapped to the spot where the ball will be spotted. I prefer the ball to come at my chest. I feel I can get it down properly just as fast and can handle bad passes more easily.

Just before the ball is snapped, give the center a target by raising your right arm about chest high. We use this raising of the arm as an indication that everyone is ready so the center can snap the ball immediately. Some clubs give a verbal signal to have the ball snapped.

Position for the snap. Give the center a big target.

As you raise your arm, lean forward as far as you can while maintaining complete balance. Bring your left arm up just as the ball is snapped. By leaning forward you will get the ball as quickly as possible, thus giving yourself more time to adjust the laces and place the ball properly.

When receiving the snap, keep your fingers loose, arms relaxed, and "look" the ball right into your hands. As the ball hits your hands your arms should recoil, and in one motion bring the ball to the mark. The laces should be facing toward the center of the goal posts. If the snap was bad and you're unable to get the laces facing directly away from the kicker, at least make sure they aren't facing him. If he hits the laces the kicks won't be true in flight. If the snap is a bad one, try and stop it from getting by you. If you can keep the ball in front of you there is still a chance you can get it down so that the kicker can make an attempt at a kick. If you can't pick the ball up, jump on it to prevent the opposing team from recovering it.

If you fumble the snap or have a bad one on an extra point, pick the ball up and try to run the point in. When it looks like you aren't going to make it, throw the ball into the end zone in the direction of one of your men. He might catch the pass and save the point. *Only do this on extra points, not field goals!*

The best way to get the lacing facing forward is by spinning the ball. As you spot the ball, put your left hand behind the ball and pull it toward you. As you bring your hand away, spin it so the laces are facing properly. Use your forefinger to hold the ball at its upper point. Some holders use their palms to hold the ball, but I find that my thumb gets in the way, so I use my forefinger. Don't exert too much pressure down on the ball; just use enough to keep the ball in place. If you exert too much pressure you'll be cutting down the distance the ball can travel.

The reason I hold with my right hand is so that my arm will not stop the follow-through of the kicker and my hand can swing away freely.

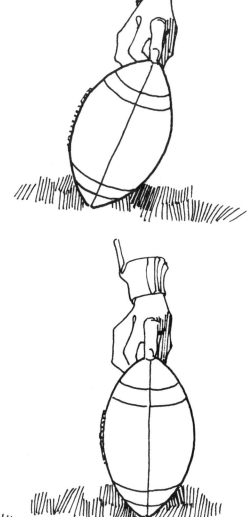

At What Angle Should the Ball be Placed?

The angle the ball is placed at is entirely up to the kicker. He will want the ball set the way he can get the most power and lift in his kick. Some of the different angles are shown.

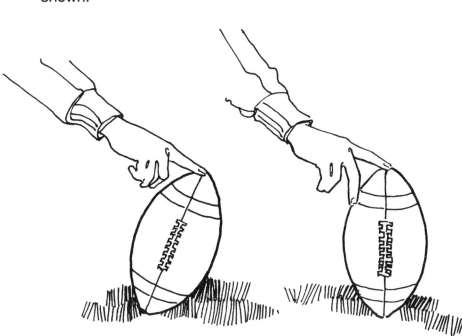

After the ball is down properly, get your head and body out of the way. If you are too close to the ball, the kicker is forced to compensate by bringing his leg across his body instead of straight through. This is especially true of kickers who approach the ball straight on. The result from such a hold is usually a missed kick.

Watch the kicker meet the ball. Don't raise your head to see if the kick is good—the crowd will tell you!

One of the reasons quarterbacks hold is to confuse the defense, as the quarterback represents a threat of a possible pass. If the defense is aware that the quarterback could possibly throw, they won't rush as many men. This cuts down the possibility of having the kick blocked and increases the chance of a successful kick.

The position of the laces. Keeping the laces away from the kicker.

9 How To Coach a Quarterback

The quarterback is the most important player on your team, and if you teach him properly, he'll make your job much easier.

Don't worry about his size. People like Bill Kilmer, Fran Tarkenton, and Russ Jackson have all made it, and they're barely six feet tall.

Make sure your quarterback is a leader. He must demonstrate his leadership ability in practice as well as in games. Boys can develop leadership if you give them a sense of responsibility.

Another very important characteristic is self-confidence. You can build this in a boy as easily as destroy it. If he deserves praise, give it to him; we all like to hear how well we are doing. On the other hand, correct him if he is wrong.

Stance

The stance is a key part of quarterbacking. If the quarterback doesn't line up the same way every time, the defense will be able to tell in advance the direction a play will go—for instance, if he lines up with his right foot a little further back when he will be going to his right and vice versa. Little things like these are a dead giveaway to the opposing defense.

Before practice, get your quarterbacks together and have them work on their stances. Make sure that they stand erect, heads up, feet about shoulder width apart. Their weight should be on the balls of their feet and the knees bent slightly. From this position they should be able to move in any direction without telegraphing the play.

Stance. Being comfortable is the key.

Cadence

The cadence is the starting signal for all teams. Your quarterbacks should call it out loud, clear, and crisp. With crowd noise, "two" could sound like "blue," and if the signal isn't enunciated, your team could well blow the play.

As your quarterback is calling signals, have him pause after every audible. This slight pause allows the rest of the team to adjust if a real change of play is called.

Audibles

Most coaches on the high school and junior levels don't use audibles. I agree with them. Boys on this level should concentrate on the fundamentals and not have to worry about audibles. Audibles might add too much pressure and cause the boy to become frustrated and, perhaps, give up the game.

At the college and professional level, audibles are a must in every offense. By the time boys have reached college, they should have learned the fundamentals and be prepared to take on this additional responsibility.

In professional football we use a very simple system of audibilization. We break down the audibles into six categories: drop-back passes, sprint-out passes, run-action passes, sweeps, off-tackles, and inside plays. (Inside plays are those run between tackles.) In each category we place two plays. Having only twelve plays in our entire audible system makes it easy for us to select a play in any situation. We don't have to waste time trying to decide which one of thirty plays to call.

The most important thing to look for when reading defenses is where your players outnumber theirs. It's a simple matter of counting bodies. Knowing where your strength is and knowing the complete blocking scheme on every play are essential to making a decision if an audible must be called. In reading defenses, teach your quarterbacks first to look over the defensive line and linebackers, then to check the alignment of the defensive secondary. After your quarterback has found a weakness, he can make a quick and accurate decision whether or not to call an audible.

These quarterback decisions are governed by the game plan, which you and the quarterback must deter-

Calling an audible at the line of scrimmage.

mine in pre-game meetings. It is important that you and he think alike. Such meetings should ensure that the quarterback does not grasp for plays, and will daily increase the efficiency of the offense. They can be formal or informal, with or without film. I suggest that your quarterback looks at films at least an hour each day during the season, so that he can pick out plays and see what defenses a team plays in certain situations.

Pivoting

The only way to become really skillful at something is to work on it every day. Good pivots are very important, as they help eliminate poor faking, missed hand-offs, and sloppy footwork. Proper pivoting and good footwork may seem like a small thing, but for every play to move along smoothly they are a must.

During each practice you'll be spending about one and a half hours executing plays. On every play you should be concentrating on the pivots.

When coaching a boy on his footwork, be sure he doesn't take false steps. If you can eliminate this problem, the rest will come with practice.

Conditioning

Quarterbacks of all ages should go through a certain conditioning program. Younger kids usually take less time to warm up than older ones.

The groin, hamstrings, and back are three areas that must be good and loose before a workout begins. Strengthening the throwing arm comes with constant exercise, such as the exercises shown in Chapter 2. Basketball is great for keeping your wind up, and it also gives you a sense of coordination, builds up the legs and wrists, and maintains a competitive spirit.

Equipment

Make sure your quarterback is well protected. The equipment he'll be wearing will be very similar to that worn by his teammates. It is important that his helmet doesn't block his vision in any way and his shoulder pads don't hamper his throwing. Be sure each piece does the job it is supposed to and completely covers the areas it should protect.

Throwing

Certain physical characteristics aid in throwing; hand size, wrist and forearm strength, and body balance are all very important. The larger a boy's hand, the easier it will be for him to grip the ball. Wrist and forearm strength will give him greater distance when passing. Proper body balance will aid in the accuracy of the passes.

Except for hand size, these physical characteristics can be built up, but the boys you choose as quarterbacks must already possess them to some degree.

Throwing Exercises

These exercises are designed to strengthen the arm and improve trajectory and accuracy.

1. Before each practice, have your quarterbacks play catch at different distances, starting at ten yards, *over* the cross-bar. This warms up their arms and makes them stress trajectory and accuracy. They should try to throw as close as possible to the bar without hitting it.

2. After their arms are loosened up, have your quarterbacks kneel on their right knee and throw the ball back and forth to one another. You should have them start at a distance of ten yards and gradually work out. The quarterback who isn't throwing should flash his hands

Throwing exercise number 5.

at intended spots of reception. The object here is to build up the arm without using the body for help. Flashing different spots of reception helps the quarterback to work on his accuracy.

After they finish about ten minutes of this exercise, have them switch knees. Always make sure they rotate the wrist outward, turn their upper body toward the receiver, follow through, and keep the ball up before delivering the pass. Stress these four main points in every throwing exercise.

The preceding two exercises should be done in the half-hour before practice. The following four exercises should be done during the breakdown period of practice.

3. Have your quarterbacks pair off and, about ten yards apart, start jogging in a clockwise circle. Have them throw the ball back and forth, working on their release, rotation of hips, and aim. As they jog they should gradually try to make the circle larger. They should always try to throw to a spot about a foot in front of the receiver's chest. After about three minutes, have them switch and jog in a counterclockwise direction, repeating the exercise for the same length of time.

4. Have a receiver stand fifteen yards upfield, between the hash mark and the sideline. The quarterback lines up on the opposite hash mark and takes or simulates a snap from center. With the proper footwork he should sprint out, throwing the ball on the run to the stationary target. The actual distance between the quarterback and receivers will depend on the age of the quarterbacks. Younger quarterbacks should be closer together; high school and college quarterbacks should be lined up as previously explained. This exercise will help your quarterbacks throw on the run, build up their arms, and improve their accuracy when throwing to a stationary target. It is also a good drill for learning how to throw a curl pattern while on the run.

5. The quarterbacks line up in the same way as for number 4, but the receiver should be on the same line as the quarterbacks in the same position he would for an actual play on the opposite hash mark.

On the snap count, the quarterback sprints out while the receiver runs various patterns, such as sidelines, flats, and flag patterns. This exercise helps build up the arm and gives the quarterback a chance to work on various throwing techniques while throwing to a moving target.

6. A very similar exercise to number 5 can be performed, using the drop-back technique; it can be used to practice both the backpedaling and the dropping back sideways methods. The quarterbacks line up on the hash, with receivers on the other hash. The receivers run various patterns, with the quarterbacks working on their drop back techniques. Watch that they drop properly, keep the ball up, release the ball higher than the shoulder, keep the off arm close to the body, rotate the wrist outward, and shift the weight from the back leg to the front.

Use these exercises at least twice a week. Rotating them during the breakdown period will give your quarterbacks a chance to build up every part of their throwing game. It also gives you a chance to keep them doing the right things.

Teach your quarterbacks to think "completion"— that is, to concentrate on where the ball is going at all times. It is easy to check the physical fundamentals, but teaching them to think completion can only come from many hours of meetings and practice.

Hand-Offs

In handing off, be sure your quarterback works from the stomach and always locks the ball into the ball carrier's stomach. Be sure he makes the hand-off in front of his line of vision and doesn't follow the play after the hand-off is made.

During each practice your quarterbacks should spend a good 45 minutes handing off; be sure they are doing it correctly.

Practice Sessions

Your practice sessions should be well organized. Accomplish what you intend to, then get off the field.

If I were to go into coaching tomorrow, here's how I would organize and run my practice sessions: First a warm-up session, then agility drills, breakdown period, time for pass offense, time for run offense, full-team time-up, then a goal-line and special plays period.

Before practice your quarterbacks should loosen up their arms and the kickers practice kicking. After doing the exercises mentioned earlier in this chapter, your quarterbacks should be good and loose. For another prepractice exercise, have them hold for extra points and field goals.

The warm-up session includes calisthenics and stretching exercises—jumping jacks, toe touches, cross-over leg stretches, sit-ups, hurdler's stretch, push-ups—finishing with jumping jacks.

The agility drills will loosen up your quarterbacks. This drill period could include three sprints of forty yards, ten yards of bear crawl, two forward rolls, and ten yards of carioca.

During the breakdown period your quarterbacks, backs, and centers work on ball handling, including stances, exchanges, pivoting, and handing off. The period should last about 30 minutes.

The next part of practice, also lasting about 30 minutes, covers your pass offense. I suggest passing first, because the quarterbacks' arms will still be loose. If the passing session takes place later in the practice, their arms might be stiff, and you'll increase the chance of a sore arm.

While working on the passing game your quarterbacks should also be concentrating on good techniques—checking to see they get a good drop, working on their timing, reading defenses, and throwing the ball properly.

The next 30 minutes are devoted to the run offense. Here your quarterbacks can polish up on their defensive recognition as well as their footwork and ball handling.

During the pass and run periods your quarterbacks have been practicing techniques and fundamentals. They have had very little pressure on them. To prepare them for actual game conditions the next 15 minutes should be devoted to full team time-up. In this time period mix up passes and running plays so your quarterback can get a real feel for his offense and become acquainted with situations he will be faced with in games. It's almost like having a controlled scrimmage.

The last 15 minutes of practice should be devoted to goal line and special plays. Putting the ball in the end zone is the true test of a quarterback. This is where the pressure really is in a game. It's easy to move the ball between the 20-yard lines, but a great quarterback can put the ball in the end zone and the points on the board.

Most teams have two or three running plays and two or three pass plays for goal-line situations. The key to success is practicing them until everyone knows them perfectly. Those 15 minutes spent on goal line work can spell the difference between success and failure.

Also included in that time period are special or trick plays. Just one or two plays like a reverse or a hitch-and-pitch are enough to have in your offense. These plays are designed to keep the defense off-guard; you'll only need to use them once every two or three games.

As you approach the day of a game you should cut down practice gradually and just have a light work-out the day before a game. During that work-out you should go over the entire game plan.

A time schedule for a typical week of the practice just outlined, assuming the game is on Saturday, would go as follows:

Monday

15 minutes warm-up
10 minutes breakdown
20 minutes pass offense
20 minutes run-off
10 minutes team time-up
 5 minutes special

Tuesday

15 minutes warm-up
15 minutes breakdown
30 minutes pass
30 minutes run
15 minutes team time-up
15 minutes goal line
 5 minutes special

Wednesday

Same as Tuesday

Thursday

15 minutes warm-up
15 minutes breakdown
20 minutes pass
20 minutes run
10 minutes team time-up
10 minutes goal line
 5 minutes special

Friday	10 minutes warm-up
	10 minutes breakdown
	30 minutes team time-up
Saturday	Game
Sunday	Mandatory report for treatment of all injuries
	Jog one mile

In the week just outlined you should have covered all teaching and coaching points. Then it is up to your quarterback to do his job and lead the team to victory. During each week stress the coaching points, and soon you will see that the constant repetition has caused the quarterback to develop the habits of moving properly.

Many boys have great potential to become quarterbacks, but it requires a joint effort by the coach and the boy to develop this potential.

Follow through.

Photo by Nate Fine

10 How To Choose a Quarterback

The quarterback is the key man in an offense. It is important that you know what he is made of before you put him in charge. The boy's background will give you some insight into the type of person he is. Factors to consider are his school marks, which will give you some idea of his intelligence; his environment, or how he was brought up, which will tell you something about the boy as a person and the type of hours he keeps. You can get some indication of his self-discipline from the hours he keeps. Knowing as much as possible about the boy will help you decide if he is quarterback material.

Ask yourself these questions when selecting a prospective quarterback.

Does He Have Natural Ability?

Because the quarterback position is one of the skilled positions on a football team, certain athletic gifts are necessary. Coordination, dexterity, and all-around quickness are three of the basic ones.

The quarterback will be required to perform movements that are unnatural for him. If he has the natural ability, the movements can be easily learned.

How Does He Throw?

Unless you have a wishbone offense, the boy's arm is a very important factor. Your offense should be shaped to suit your personnel; choosing a boy with a strong arm gives you an opportunity to diversify your pass offense. If the boy has a weak arm, you are limited to a shorter type of passing attack. However, the boy with a weaker arm can be just as effective provided his offense suits his talents.

Does He Have the Voice?

The quarterback's voice is very important. If he has a weak one, it will be difficult for his teammates to hear him

Carrying the ball properly while running.

Photo by Nate Fine

call signals over a lot of crowd noise. The team will also have trouble hearing the signals being called in the huddle. If a quarterback is upset, the team can tell by his voice when he calls the play. If it is weak and cracks they will feel uneasy and know he is upset. You can't expect the team to follow someone who shows fear in his voice.

Is He Punctual?

The presence of the quarterback is a must for meetings and practice. When he doesn't show up the entire plan is disrupted. If he is often late for practice and meetings, find out why. Usually it means he doesn't care enough about the game to make the necessary sacrifices to win. He is placing himself first and the team second. In a team game such players can cause nothing but trouble.

Does He Practice Hard?

Poor performance during games is usually the result of a poor performance during practice. Play like you practice. If he doesn't put out in practice when there is little pressure, you can bet he won't perform well when the crowd is yelling and the band is playing. As I mentioned earlier, the quarterback is the key to an offense. If he doesn't practice hard, the other players have no one to act as a catalyst. Your quarterback *must* be the leader at *all* times.

Does He Have Confidence?

In order to be a good quarterback, the boy should and must have confidence. He must be confident of his own ability, the ability of the men he plays with, and your ability as a coach. Many boys have great talent but lack confidence in some area. These are the boys who never really make it. The key is *complete* confidence.

Does He Have the Dedication to Study and Learn?

Many young men have great natural talent but lack the dedication necessary to become great athletes. Your quarterback must feel the same way you do about the game. Being on time for meetings, staying after practices to improve himself, asking questions to get a better understanding of the offense and defenses—these are all signs of a quarterback's dedication, on and off the field.

Does He Have a Competitive Spirit?

The will to win is something every athlete must have. You can usually tell the spirit of competition a boy has by watching him perform in sports other than football,

"You've got to think high to rise."

whether they are as simple as marbles or as physical as basketball. If the boy wants to win in everything he does and plays his heart out, he'll be a real asset to your ball club.

Can He Take Criticism?

Some players can't accept criticism without giving excuses for their mistakes. Sometimes their reasons are valid, but more often they can be annoying. Constant objection creates problems in communication, and there is nothing a coach hates more than a lack of communication between himself and his quarterback. Most of my coaches have followed a policy that works well: After a player is criticized, if he wants to explain why he did something, he should take it up with the coach after practice. This eliminates a lot of time-consuming discussion and keeps practice moving smoothly.

Other players will be watching how the coach handles the situation. Don't invite trouble; you and the quarterback must understand which one of you is the coach and which one is the player. If you establish this relationship with your quarterback, your team will function better.

Is He a Leader?

The quarterback must be able to take charge of the situation. On the field he should have the team working with him at all times. When he calls a play there should be no doubt in anyone's mind that the play will work. If things don't go according to plan, he must be able to improvise and turn an obvious broken play into a successful play. When the team breaks the huddle, he should jog up to the line of scrimmage. He should be willing to stay after practice and work. Other players begin to take note of these things and wonder why they aren't out there working that extra little bit.

A coach lives or dies with his quarterback. Choosing a boy who has great leadership ability can make your job a lot easier.

Is He a Quitter?

It is easy to play quarterback when your team is winning and everything is going fine. When you get into a tight situation in which you need to score and the pressure is building, some quarterbacks will give up and quit trying. They'll take the easy way out, resorting to hand-offs and hoping that the halfback or fullback will break loose for a touchdown and bail them out.

Everybody has a bad day. If one's arm isn't sharp he'll miss completing a few passes by just inches. But one key play can spark life back into the team, and if the quarterback remembers this, he can more easily overcome his

"Congratulations Mo." Mark Mosley, MVP, National Football League, 1982.

Photo by Paul Schmick

problems. Continuing to make the same mistakes and not tryng to correct them means he lacks the determination and desire necessary to become a great quarterback. "When the going gets tough, the tough get going."

Is He Physically Durable?

Quarterbacks must be able to take a certain amount of punishment. Football is a contact sport, and the quarterback will get bounced around quite frequently. He must be durable enough to last a full season. When you have developed an attack for a certain quarterback and he gets hurt often, you'll constantly have to be changing your game plan, reducing the effectiveness of your offense.

"High school buddies." Drew Pearson and I talk about old times.

This is why most professional teams carry at least two good quarterbacks. I have always felt that the key to being a successful quarterback is staying healthy.

Is He Respected by His Teammates?

This is the most important attribute of a quarterback. If he is respected by his teammates, he can lead them to victory. Players, and players alone, are the best judges of quarterbacks. The media formulate opinions about them; sometimes they are right, sometimes not. But other ball-players—the offensive linemen, backs, and receivers—know how the quarterback handles himself in different situations. They know if they can count on him for the big play.

The quarterback must be a coach on the field. He must know everybody's assignment on every play. If a play doesn't work, he should know why. By having this knowledge, he can speak with authority in the huddle, and the other ball players will listen.

Having one of the players come up to me after a game and say, "Nice game, Joe," means more to me than any award I could receive. This guy knows what it's like on a field—we've been through it together.

These are some of the qualifications I would look for if I had to choose a quarterback. Younger quarterbacks won't be as strong in some points as older ones. The younger ones will improve with age; the older ones should possess most of the talents, but need polishing.

If you can find a quarterback who possesses these qualifications, not necessarily in the order listed, he'll be the best around and the type of person capable of leading a team to a championship.

The more you know about the boy, the better equipped you'll be to work with him. Offenses should be developed around your personnel. If the quarterback has certain talents, you should use them in the best way possible. While you are developing an offense to suit his strong talents, you should be developing exercises to strengthen his weaknesses.

APPENDICES

Appendix A
Equipment Checklist

When you are finished with your equipment, hang it up to dry. The equipment you buy will last you a long time provided you take care of it, so make a habit of checking the items.

Shoes

Put them in a well-ventilated area so that they can dry easily. Be sure the spikes are tight and that none are missing. Check the inside sole; make sure the rivets aren't coming through the sole insert.

Use new laces as soon as the old ones start to get worn.

Thigh and Knee Pads

Sometimes the plastic or cardboard inside gets cracked; if this happens change the pads immediately. Make sure the pads cover the areas they should.

Hip Pads

Be sure that the pockets aren't ripped; check for tears and fix them without delay. Adjust the pads so that they fit comfortably and protect the hips and tailbone completely.

Shoulder Pads

Check the straps to see if they are losing their elasticity. If the rivets holding the pads in place are loose, replace the shoulder pads. The laces on both sides of the pads should be tight.

Helmet

The helmet is the most important piece of equipment, as it protects your head and neck from serious injury. When checking the helmet, be sure that the suspension is tight and that there aren't any cracks in the helmet casing. The face mask should be tight and in the proper place. The chin strap should have no cracks and should keep your helmet in place.

Appendix B
Pass Patterns: Terminology

The following is the terminology used to describe different pass patterns for backs, outside receivers, and inside receivers. The illustrations included are suggested ways to run the patterns.

Outside Receiver Patterns

1. Go   Release hard off the line, without any fake, and try to outrun the defender down the field.

2. Post   Release hard off the line for ten yards; plant your outside foot and break in at a 45-degree angle. The actual angle of the break will be determined by the field position and defensive alignment. Look for the ball over your inside shoulder.

3. Flag   Release hard off the line for ten yards; plant your inside foot and break at about a 45-degree angle for the sidelines. The actual angle of the break will be determined by the field position and defensive alignment.

4. Delay   Drop back one step, allowing the inside receivers to clear out the area, then break into the open area.

5. Slant-In   Release hard off the line for three yards, cut at about a 45-degree angle, gaining depth according to the linebacker's drop.

6. Hitch   Release hard off the line for five yards; plant your outside foot and turn inside, looking for the ball.

7. Sideline   Release hard off the line for ten yards; plant your inside foot and square out. Look for the ball over your inside shoulder.

Outside Receiver Patterns

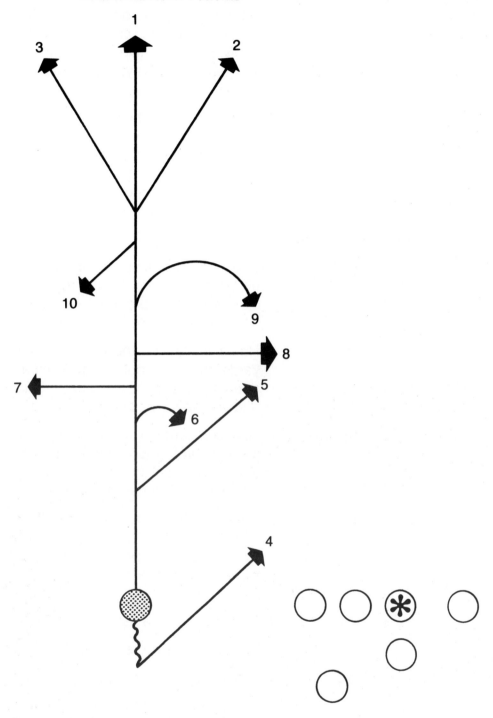

Outside Receiver Patterns

8. Break-In   Release hard off the line for fifteen yards; plant your outside foot, then square in sharply. Don't slow down. Look for the ball over your inside shoulder.

| 9. Curl | Release hard off the line for eighteen yards; plant your outside foot and turn to the inside, creating an open throwing lane between you and the quarterback. Always come back to the ball. |
| 10. Comeback | Release hard off the line for eighteen yards; plant your inside foot and come back to the outside to fifteen yards, always trying to keep yourself between the defender and the ball. |

Inside Receiver Patterns

1. Delay	Drop back, setting up in a pass blocking position, letting the area clear out. Then break into the open area looking quickly for the ball.
2. Stop	Release hard off the line up to ten yards; then turn outside and find an opening between the quarterback and yourself. Don't drift too far out.
3. Drag Out	Release hard off the line to seven yards; plant your inside foot and square out, looking over your inside shoulder for the ball.
4. Curl	Release hard off the line to a depth of twelve yards; plant your outside foot and turn inside to an open area between the quarterback and yourself.
5. Post	Same as outside receiver.
6. Center	Same as outside receiver.
7. Flag	Same as outside receiver.
8. Go	Release hard off the line straight up the field. After clearing the linebacker, look for the ball.
9. Slant-Out	Release hard off the line for three yards; plant your inside foot and square out, looking for the ball over your inside shoulder.

Inside Receiver Patterns

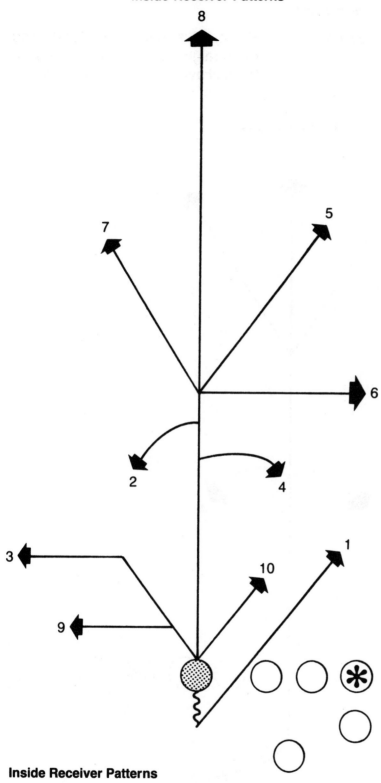

Inside Receiver Patterns

10. Quick   Release hard off the line at a 45-degree angle to the inside, looking quickly for the ball.

Backs' Patterns

1. Swing — Release just outside the tackle and run straight up the field, looking for the ball over your inside shoulder.

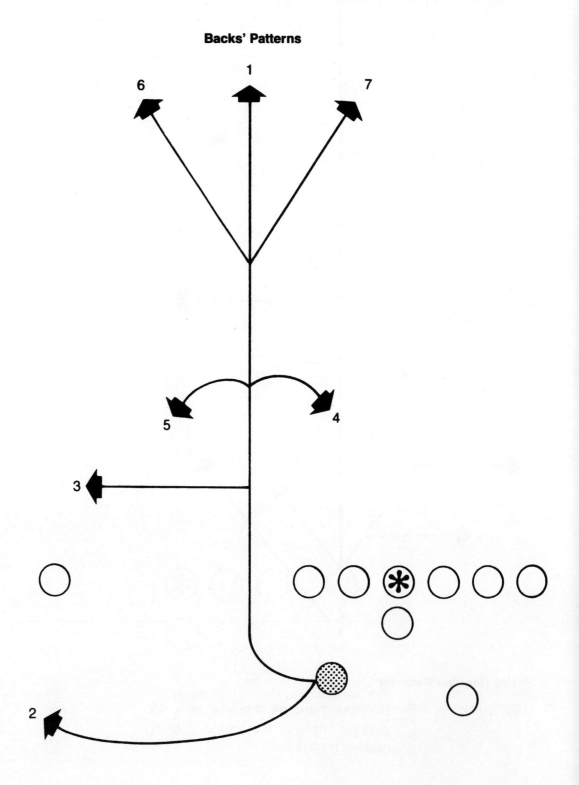

Backs' Patterns

2. Flare   Push off with the inside foot, losing ground, and always look back at the quarterback for the ball.

3. Flat   Release outside the tackle and go upfield for five yards. Then plant your inside foot and square out, looking for the ball over your inside shoulder.

4. Hook   Run a swing; at seven yards plant your outside foot, then turn and hook to the inside.

5. Stop   Run a swing, stop at seven yards, and turn to the outside.

6. Flag   Run a swing and at ten yards break at a 45-degree angle out. The angle at which you actually break will be determined by the field position and defensive alignment.

7. Post   Run a swing and a ten yards break at a 45-degree angle to the inside. The actual angle at which you break will be determined by the field position and the defensive alignment.

Appendix C
The Eight Basic Differences between U.S. and Canadian Professional Football

1. Number of Downs

In the U.S. game there are four downs to make ten yards. In the Canadian game there are three downs.

2. Number of Players

There are eleven players on the defensive and offensive units in the U.S. version. In the Canadian game, there are twelve. The twelfth man is usually a slot back on offense and a defensive halfback or rover on defense.

The Most Commonly Used Offensive and Defensive Lineups

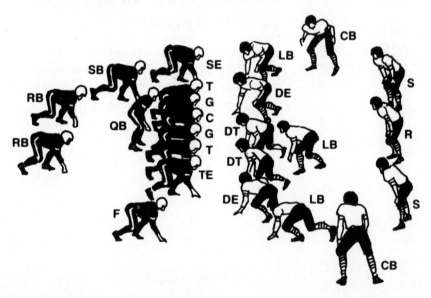

RB	Running back	**T**	Tackle	**DT**	Defensive Tackle
QB	Quarterback	**G**	Guard	**LB**	Linebacker
F	Flanker	**C**	Center	**CB**	Cornerback
SE	Split End	**DE**	Defensive End	**S**	Safety
TE	Tight End	**SB**	Slot Back	**R**	Rover

3. Distance between Offensive and Defensive Linemen

In the U.S. game, defensive linemen are allowed to line up almost nose to nose with the offensive linemen, with only the length of the football serving as a neutral zone. In the Canadian game, the defensive linemen must be one yard away from the ball, creating a larger neutral zone.

4. Point after Touchdown

In the U.S. game, the ball is scrimmaged from the second yard line after a touchdown. In the Canadian game, the ball is scrimmaged from the ten yard line for the extra point.

5. Backs in Motion

In U.S. football, only one back is allowed in motion, and only in a lateral or backward direction. In the Canadian game, all of the backs are allowed to be in motion—forward, backward, or sideways—before the ball is snapped.

6. Game Time

In the U.S. game, a team is allowed three time-outs in each half, and the clock is stopped if an incomplete pass is thrown, the ball carrier is knocked out of bounds, or a first down is made. There is also a two-minute warning given before the end of the second and fourth quarters.

In the Canadian game, there are no time-outs and the game is played with running time. There is a three-minute warning given at the end of the second and fourth quarters. During these three minutes, the clock is stopped in the same way as in the U.S. game.

7. Punt Returns

The punt returner in the U.S. game has three options when fielding a punt. He can call for a fair catch, let the ball bounce and roll dead, or field it and return it with his teammates blocking for him. If he elects to let the punt roll into the end zone, it is blown dead and brought out and scrimmaged from the twenty-yard line.

In the Canadian game, the punt returner can do just one thing: catch the punt and return it. However, the kicking team, other than the kicker, must allow the punt returner five yards to field the ball. If a member of the kicking team gets closer than five yards, a no-yards penalty of ten yards is assessed against the kicking team.

If the ball is bouncing around and the kicker recovers it, his team retains possession with an automatic first down.

A punt or missed field goal attempt going into the end zone must be returned out of the end zone, or a single point is awarded to the kicking team. The ball is then brought out to, and scrimmaged from, the 25-yard line.

8. Field

The difference in the fields is the most striking feature between the U.S. and Canadian games—the U.S. field being much smaller. The dimensions of the U.S. field are: 100 yards × 53 yards, with 10-yard end zones. The Canadian field: 110 yards × 65 yards, with 25-yard end zones.

A Superimposition of U.S. Field on a Canadian Field

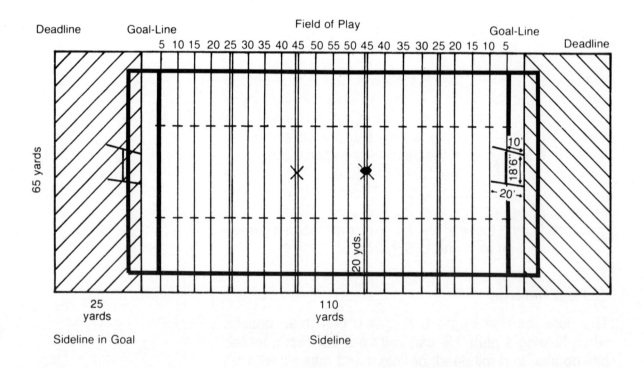

Diagram labels: Deadline, Goal-Line, Field of Play, Goal-Line, Deadline. Yard markers: 5 10 15 20 25 30 35 40 45 50 55 50 45 40 35 30 25 20 15 10 5. 65 yards (left side vertical). 10', 18'6", 20' (right side). 20 yds. (center). 25 yards / Sideline in Goal. 110 yards / Sideline.

"Putting it all together..."

Photo by Notre Dame Univ. Sports Info. Dept.

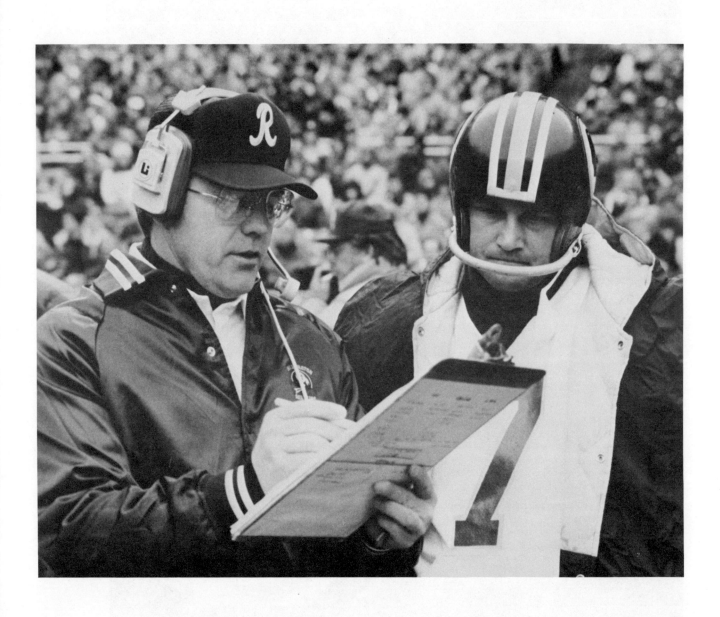